*To the Lover of my **soul**.*

Gift. De Pate Sanchez Donation 2/18/2016

What people are saying about

Here is good news—*you are being divinely romanced*. If you have ever wondered how to have a passionate relationship with the Lord, then *Made for More* is the book for you. Irini Fambro's honest and transparent approach is fresh and impacting.

Pastor Debbie Morris
Pastor of Pink, Women's Ministry | Gateway Church
Co-Author of *The Blessed Marriage* with Pastor Robert Morris
Author of *The Blessed Woman*

This book unwraps the bare essence of God's pursuit and strips off the words and traditions that have clothed God's Bridegroom passion toward His bride.

Bob Hamp
Executive Pastor of Pastoral Care | Gateway Church
Author of *Think Differently Live Differently: Keys to a Life of Freedom*

Sex has been defined by our culture for too long. Everything in the natural is a reflection of the spiritual. Watch as Irini unfolds how this God-given gift originates with our Bridegroom. *Jesus is the lover of my soul*—often quoted, but less often experienced. Jesus truly does long to become first our Savior, then our Friend and over time, our Lover. Through her own personal story, Irini shares her journey into true intimacy, the bride becoming the lover of her Bridegroom.

Nancy Houston
Licensed Christian Sex Therapist
Associate Pastor of Unity, Married Life | Gateway Church

For too long, the church has kept relationship with Jesus locked up in a safe, comfortable friendship. In *Made for More*, Irini Fambro kicks us out of our comfort zones, challenging us to go further than ever with the Lord. This book will ask you to push beyond what you've always thought of as intimacy, expanding your boundaries and your thinking. Get ready for more!

Alan Smith
Pastor of Freedom Ministries | Gateway Church
Author of *Unveiled*

The truths in *Made for More* are relevant and life changing, and really opened my eyes to a different perspective on my relationship with God. The principles are dynamic and will meet you where you are—and take you to a whole new level. I would recommend this book to every one, no matter how young or old you are.

Elaine Fisher
Speaker

made for more

Arini Tamfro

ISBN 978-1-62050-195-5 North American Edition
Library of Congress Control Number: 2012906227

Visit www.bemorethan.com for additional ministry information.

Cover Design by Irini Fambro
Back Cover Photo by Delilah Richey
Four Oaks Photo by Katie Coiner
Edited by Nancy Smith | AuthorityPressOnline.com
Layout Design by Brandon Day | ThinkTreeMedia.com

Printed in the U.S.A.

contents

acknowledgements

I start with whom I dedicated this book to, the Lover of my soul. While I was running, You called me to draw in. I kept my running shoes on thinking that we would draw in for a moment and then continue to run together. After the shoes came off, life began. As I ran, I knew You. But now, as You have drawn me in—I *know* you so much more deeply. *Place me like a seal over your heart, like a seal on your arm. For love is as strong as death, its jealousy as enduring as the grave. Love flashes like fire, the brightest kind of flame* (Song of Solomon 8:6, NLT).

To my husband, Kenneth, the love of my life. You are the one who heard every thought in this book before it was ever written. I am grateful for our late night talks, the faith-stretching "what-ifs," and your unending belief in me. I am a better Irini because of you.

To my children, Kalila and Warren. One day you will read this book. My desire is that it will only be a reflection of what you have seen to be true in my own life.

It was in conceiving, carrying, laboring and nurturing you two that I saw a glimpse into a heavenly reality.

To my family who have nurtured and grown me in my faith. The love and sacrifice that you gave, and continue to give, is empowering. I love you dearly and am thankful for the grace that you have constantly given me along the journey.

To my friends, I wish I could name you all. How do you know you fit this category? The pages of this book will have you reminiscing about a conversation we had at a coffee shop, at church, in the parking lot, at my home, over the phone ... you remember it. It probably shocked you at first, but then you let me keep talking. This book is the sifting out of all those conversations. Thank you for letting me speak, think and share all that God was doing these past nine years.

To Bob Hamp and Nancy Smith, thank you for pushing me so that *Made for More* is better than when I handed it to you. Your insight, your faith and your boldness have carried me as I have labored to birth this book. I am so thankful God chose you two to run the last leg of the journey with me.

foreword

It is impossible to read the Bible beyond a cursory glance without beginning to pick up on how God pictures His relationship with the human race. His language is always about family relationship, and most consistently, He describes our relationship with the terms Bride and Bridegroom. It sounds sweet, until we begin to take it literally. Then it can become a little uncomfortable.

Irini Fambro has taken it literally, engaging the discomfort head on and without apology. I like that about her, and I like that about her book.

Having been raised in a non-religious environment, I have often observed how we as believers wrap our words and ideas in tradition and familiarity. Nothing can rob us of the depth and breadth of deep encounter more than tradition and familiarity. It is the death knell of many marriages, and can be the signal of a dying relationship with God when that which is designed to inflame our soul becomes common and mundane.

This book unwraps the bare essence of God's pursuit and strips off the words and traditions that have concealed God's Bridegroom passion toward His bride.

Irini approaches God's pursuit of our hearts and God's intention to engage us with the freshness of a newlywed. She takes God's Bride and Bridegroom metaphor at face value and pushes us all toward the obvious, yet squirm-inducing, conclusions of this imagery.

Central topics like identity, destiny, passion and spiritual warfare are all tied to the levels of intimacy that are implied in the bridegroom paradigm. To shy away from this metaphor would be to shy away from the central issues of our life in Christ and our walk with Him. I am glad that Irini has not been shy.

Written not like an academic, but as a lover, Irini has given this book more the feel of a memoir of a love story than an exposition of ideas. And honestly, to approach the topic of love and intimacy through intellect and cognition so deeply separates method and message that the message would cease to be clear.

Irini's personal love story becomes an opportunity for us all to be reminded in the deep places of our soul that we are still being pursued by a Lover; and that all He has ever wanted with us is still what He wants, and is what He will want for all eternity.

Don't let the ideas scare you; or if they do, don't let them chase you away. Avoid God's intimate pursuit and you miss out on the foundation of all the riches of a life lived by design. Instead, let Perfect Love do its work and cast out fear.

If you haven't already, join the Lover's game and let *Made for More* stir in you the reminder of all you were made for and all that can be yours in the chambers of the King of the Universe. I am grateful that Irini wrote this book, and by the end I think you will be too.

Bob Hamp
Executive Pastor of Pastoral Care | Gateway Church
Author of *Think Differently Live Differently:*
    Keys to a Life of Freedom

introduction

Have you ever felt like there was more out there? More than the rat race. More than the casual relationships we settle for. More than ladders of expectation, where we climb from rung to rung, hoping to somehow reach … something. The longer we journey with God, the more we find ourselves hoping for more, dreaming of some utopian place. And while we may make small changes to try and shift our reality, somehow life with God still looks the same. Our lives revert to the same old ebb and flow, and look much the way they did before we met Him.

We discover that the rat race remains, only now it's on a different course marked by spiritual "highs" and Bible studies. The ladders of expectation have just been picked up and placed on a different wall. Ladders that lead to nowhere, in boxes that limit our destinies.

There has to be more than this. I have to believe a greater depth can exist in my relationship with God, and yet I know that I am not capable of manufacturing that depth on my own. I want an intimacy with God that goes beyond a casual flirting—but doesn't get lost in marital duty. I want intimacy that takes me past the known to the unknown.

Too much of my relationship with Him seems manmade, and looks just like that of many other followers in this world. Why is that? How many relationships do you know that look exactly the same? How boring that must be for God; no wonder it gets old for us. We are all unique, from our looks to our thoughts to our passions. And yet the way I study the Bible, journal and pray makes me look like a reproduction of the latest Western Judeo-Christian mold—just another cookie cutout. When does it become *my* relationship with God, not based on what might be considered culturally correct?

If you're not at this point, this will be just another book on your shelf, another badge on your spiritual sash; or worse, another rung up a ladder leading to a cardboard cutout dream. But if, like me, you are frustrated, then let me also warn you that this is not a concisely packaged how-to book that is going to revive you, or bring you out of your dry places. What follows are pages filled with an image that we brush up against, but often are too boxed-in to delve into too deeply. Do we dare to look closely at this image? What about embracing the things that lead us to belief in the first place? What would that do? How would we feel? What would we have to face?

Let's watch as questions meet their answers.

chapter one | **pursuit**

When I met my husband, I was a racist—and yet he pursued me anyway. That statement is a shocking one, I know, and Kenneth loves to open with that when people ask how we met. As much as we laugh about it, the sad part is that it was true.

My dad took a job as a professor at the University of Alabama, right after I was born in New York. While being a professor at Columbia was exciting, he decided he would much rather raise his girls in a "calmer" place than New York City. And calm it was. Alabama is beautiful. The town is beautiful. The neighborhood is beautiful. What I didn't think was beautiful was my family.

Now take a deep breath. I don't mean I thought we looked ugly; we were just different than everybody else. Let me put it this way, everyone in my neighborhood was white and I wasn't. Trying to explain that you're Egyptian in a town in Alabama is not as easy as it sounds. As I grew up, I was often asked if I was white, black or mixed. Needless to say, I never initiated a dialogue about race. I didn't like being different, or anything that would accentuate it.

I'm Egyptian—and Kenneth is African-American. In our town, I was already a few rungs down on the social ladder; but he was "beneath" me, or so I thought. I was a racist, stiff-arming him because of our culture, and yet he pursued me anyway. He initiated, and boy, did I respond. I didn't know what I wanted at the time, but I am so thankful he did.

I love being pursued. When I'm being pursued, I am the object of someone's attention. (Did I mention I like attention too?) Pursuit takes time, effort and planning, which means I'm worth it. Why do you think Jerry kept living in the same house as Tom? Or why did Road Runner keep letting Coyote get so close? There was always a smirk on their faces as they ended their shows, free from the clutches of their pursuer. They liked being pursued. Few people really like to be the pursuer. Some may love the challenge, the game—but only if they think they're going to get what they're after. But who wants to pursue the impossible, let alone something that has the potential to fail?

God does. It's odd, actually, to realize that God is pursuing me. All along I felt like I was pursuing Him, trying to figure Him out, hoping to finally arrive at the point where I "found God." But what I really found was that everything I was doing was merely a response to *His* pursuit. I was only answering His beckoning. I still believe in free will, but God seems to make it hard not to choose Him. And that's just what my prayers, my time in His Word, my thoughts about Him, say: *I choose you.*

I love being chosen. I mean, who really wants to be the last one chosen on a kickball team? I never wanted to be picked first; that entailed too much responsibility. And since last was such a bad option, fourth or fifth looked really good. Not too much pressure and yet not a "loser" sign across my forehead either. Being chosen says I'm worth it. Or maybe it means I've met the current minimum standard required. Either way, I am not alone; I am part of something bigger than myself. Sometimes it's a team and sometimes it's just a partnership, but at least it's not just me.

Being chosen in the middle means that someone has chosen me over another. And that is what I really want to know, right? That at least I am better than somebody else? We won't admit it, but we don't compare ourselves to the Son of God, we compare ourselves to the son of Sue or Jim or someone else— someone we can seem "better than." But that's part of our humanity. My friend says, "Competitiveness is our way of proving our value." I'm not as competitive physically as I am intellectually. I don't have to be the smartest person in the room, but I won't be the dumbest. When I applied for a PhD program and did not get in, it wounded me deeply, ripping away what I had built up for so many years.

Each year I had made a mental tally mark by moments when I was chosen and when I was not.

Unfortunately, I had been marking since elementary school.

Elementary School:	*"I like your dress.* *Do you want to play?"* Tally Mark
Junior High:	*"I like your parties.* *Want to be friends?"* Tally Mark
High School:	*"I like how you look.* *Want to date?"* Tally Mark
College:	*"I like how you think.* *Want to be in leadership?"* Tally Mark

By the time I had reached the point of applying for my doctorate, I thought I had moved past my little markings. When I applied, I placed everything I had on the scale: my 3.8 grade point average, my ethnicity, my personality, my passions, my experience, my time and my energy. I asked my husband, myself (three months pregnant) and my dog to move from Alabama to Texas. I laid it all out there. So it wasn't just a program that I didn't get into, it was what I thought was the path to my destiny. Not being chosen can be very damaging—just as being chosen can be very powerful.

There is power in our choices as well. Who we say yes to is just as important as who we say no to. We so deeply desire to be chosen that we often jump at any offer. But God extended His offer to us long before we took our first breath. He is the one who designed our ability to choose, our free will, to

Who we say yes to is just as important as who we say no to.

empower us. Do you believe that God wants us to be powerful? So why aren't we?

Many of the Church's evangelical initiatives today are geared toward one thing: a response. This should sound exciting, since God is courting and calling us back to Him. But many times, that's where it stops. A person finally responds to God—and then hits the "pause" button. We bookmark the moment and move on.

I grew up in a time when getting a response was the main focus in the church. We had many Wednesday nights (yes, I went to church in the middle of the week too) that ended with some kind of altar call. We nailed our sins to the cross—literally (we wrote them on paper). We burned things in campfires. We even had the words changed to *Achy Breaky Heart, Hey Jude, Mr. Postman* and *La Bamba* all in the hopes that someone, anyone, would respond to Jesus. "Because if you don't give your heart, your achy breaky heart, I just don't think He'll understand. But if you give your heart, your achy breaky heart, He'll take you to the Promised Land." I know, you're asking yourself just how true this story is; want the chord chart?

I became addicted to altar calls, and I never seemed to move past them. "Square one" was where I made my home. If I was confused, if I was scared, if I was uncertain, if I … I just thought my first response wasn't good enough and that I needed to respond again.

What we fail to realize, what I failed to realize, is that we were intended to respond once—and then every day. The moment at the coffee shop, or a friend's home, or at the altar—that's a great start, but it is not all God intends for us. He wants us to respond to Him the next day, and the next … the next week … the next month … until we see Him face to face. But for most of us, our experience was an event we point back to, the part of our testimony when we say things got better—and maybe our first and last known response to God. But God designed it differently: we were made for more.

His design included daily interaction. Every morning, the Israelites had to wait for their manna (meal) that God sent down from heaven for them. They weren't allowed to store it up for tomorrow, either. Words like *take up [your] cross daily* (Luke 9:23), *give us this day our daily bread* (Matthew 6:1); they are all red letter words in Scripture that tell us of God's economy—an economy that values the daily over the momentary, the process over the arrival. I'm not saying God never wants us to get anywhere. But sometimes we get so caught up with the end that we forget the journey. And let's be honest; more of our lives are spent in the process than in the arrival.

But this journey was intended to change us. Our constant responses are intended to do something, to have some kind of impact. And what happens as we respond back to Him? We take up our cross daily, knowing that it leads to death (Luke 9:23). Sounds romantic, right? As we develop new relationships, we look for the ones that will allow us to be who we really are. But think about it: our greatest relationships are the ones that have changed us in some way, shape or form. And aren't the best relationships the ones that truly help you become who you are created to be, not allowing you to stay the way you are?

As I write this, I am enjoying my thirteenth year of marriage. A lot of things have happened in thirteen years. Comparing who I was then to who I am now, I can see that a lot of me has died in those years. Before I was married, my mornings were my mornings, my days were my days and my nights were my nights. I didn't like it then, but I see the upside of it now. I could get up and eat breakfast and not think about anyone else. If I forgot to plan for dinner, it didn't matter; I always had cereal or *Ramen* noodles. But to make room for Kenneth, I had to give up some mental and physical space for him. I couldn't just think of me in the morning, I had to think about us. I couldn't spend money and not think about how it affected our budget. I laid down some of my thoughts, my time and my wants to make room for him. But it did not leave me without hope. My goals, my dreams and my desires have all died and become something new and better with Kenneth. God wants the same in us: day by day, little by little, we die.

There is power in our response to His pursuit. The constant variable—that which doesn't change within the equation—is God's initiative: He never changes. He never stops pursuing us. He never gives up on us. But what can change in the equation is our response. Everyday we respond to Him through our words, how we spend our time, whom we speak to and who we ignore, our checkbooks, the phone calls we make, the coffee we share with a friend, the time we carve out for His Word. Our choices are powerful. They add up. And when we respond daily, so does He. *Blessed be the Lord, who* _daily_ *bears our burden, The God who is our salvation* (Psalm 68:19). God doesn't desire a response out of guilt, duty or fear. We respond because of His pursuit, because of His love for us, because of our love for Him.

If you want to know why we aren't seeing the power of God in our lives, look at our day-to-day choices. Oh, we are great in the big events, the once-a-week moments; but what about the daily? Look at the first church: *And day by day continuing with one mind in the temple, and breaking bread from house to house, they were taking their meals together with gladness and sincerity of heart, praising God, and having favor with all people* (Acts 2:46-47). What was the result of their response? *And the Lord was adding to their number day by day those who were being saved* (v. 47). And did He do this just once? No. *So the churches were being strengthened in the faith, and were increasing in number daily* (Acts 16:5).

God is pursuing you. He wants you to answer, because your answer opens the door to a whole new world. Your choices are powerful: for better or worse, they can open or shut doors. They can free you or hold you captive. But what if your response (or lack thereof) is limiting you from experiencing more with Him? God will not move where He has not been invited to move. What has been your response to God lately? What have your thoughts, actions and words said to Him this week? Do you want more? It's your choice.

chapter two | **courting**

Of all the gifts that I have received, there is one that still makes me smirk. Kenneth and I had just moved from Alabama to Texas, during our first year of being parents. I had stepped out of doing junior high ministry to stay at home with my daughter, but at the church we attended, I was hired part-time to pastor the college ministry. I was desperate. I wanted to do ministry again. I had yet to realize that my identity was still wrapped up in what I did so I started to "work" again. Part of the time was in the office and the other part I did from home. Kenneth was so affirming in this season of dissatisfaction.

Around this time, my birthday arrived. Now you have to understand that my birthday is a bit of an issue. I may still need counseling for it. My birthday is November 23rd. It sounds innocent, but in reality it is a martyr's birthday. When you are born the week of Thanksgiving, your birthday just gets caught in the wave of another holiday. You never really celebrate it well. You either celebrate it early, or you just make mention of it on the day and move on. (Did I mention my anniversary is November 20th?) My sister was so good at making my birthday special. She planned numerous surprise birthday parties for me. I was spoiled, and Kenneth had a lot to live up to.

This particular birthday he decided he was going to *really* come through with … the perfect gift. He was so excited about this gift. I remember the night that he gave it to me. We had just put our daughter down for the night (so we hoped) and as we sat on the couch, Kenneth was grinning from ear-to-ear. With excitement in his voice he said, "Do you want your birthday present early?" Of course I did! So he made me close my eyes and stick out my hands. Closing your eyes and waiting with your hands open is a dramatic set-up. I had great expectations.

As he laid the gift in my hands, there was a weight to it. I had no idea what it was. I opened my eyes to find a gift we would enjoy laughing about in the future; but for now, it was no laughing matter.

"A docking station," I said in confusion and disbelief (but with a hint of gratitude, or so I like to think). "A docking station. It's a docking station."

"Yes, honey, it's a docking station, why do you keep saying what it is over and over again? Don't you like it?"

"Of course I like it, you picked it."

"You don't like it."

"Yes I do. I can't wait to dock my computer in it."

"I just thought it would be awesome for work so you can just slide your laptop in and out of it with ease."

"It's great. A docking station."

To make a long story short, on the actual day of my birthday Kenneth went to the store and bought me two purses—he wanted me to have a choice. He is so good to me. For those of you who are feeling for Kenneth right now, it's okay, he laughs about it too. I mean really, it was a docking station.

Gifts are a funny thing; they can take you so many different directions. Some holidays and celebrations you remember by the gifts and the person that bought them. But all of us know that a gift means more when you know the heart of the giver. Many gifts have been forgiven based on that simple knowledge. What if I told you that you had a gift waiting for you? And what if that gift was designed specifically with you in mind? Even better, what if you could have it right now?

Walk into a room with me. A purposefully designed room, with corners of cozy light mixed with peaceful darkness. The back doors are open to capture the view of the waters meeting the shore. The scent of jasmine climbing the walls outside as it mixes with the roses arranged throughout the room draws you further in. On the veranda, you find a selection of delectable fruits and other inviting treats to enjoy. Two chairs are set out, ready to embrace the moments to come.

As you begin to look closer, you become

overwhelmed by the night sky. Have all these stars always existed? Did a few million just get added to the sky? You can hear the hum of the crickets and the small chirpings of birds settling in for the night. This must be paradise, you think. And it was.

God created man. He made light and darkness, waters and land, plants and fruits, stars and the animals ... all for man. Why the effort? God wanted more than a friend, more than a co-worker—He wanted a lover. Love makes us do strange things. Love makes us want to go over the top for someone, to find that perfect gift.

Those days of creation were used to provide something more than just function. Function would have looked like a lamp, a chair and a refrigerator. But function wasn't His only objective; God had His lover on His mind. He was thinking of a place for you and I to walk in the cool of the day with Him. He imagined the conversations, the smiles, the laughs ... the love that would be shared. Love makes us want to give our best, not because we have to, but because we want to.

God wanted you. He desires you. If you think a diamond is impressive, how about God making the world for you? And then He didn't just make the world for you; He gave you dominion over it. Go, rule over the animals, own every plant ... and while you're at it, name all of them—they're yours! Then our Lover sat back and looked at everything, and what was His comment? Not that it was good; the sky, the sea, the land, the animals—that was good. But when we became a part of the picture, He said *it was very good* (Genesis 1:31).

God could have made us in so many different ways. He could have drawn us in His image and then caused that image to come to life. To be honest, He could have just thought about making man and then man would exist. But that's not how it happened. God made man from the dust with His hands and breathed His breath into man's body, bringing life.

Talk about an intimate moment. God used his hands to form Adam. Every hair, every form, every detail was intentional. And then He took it to another level and breathed into him. He must have been really close to man to have His breath enter his body. What was inside of God was now inside of man.

God's love pushed past function and operated in extravagance. After He created Adam, He placed man in a beautiful garden filled with *every tree that is pleasing to sight and good for food* (Genesis 1:9). And then He said, *It is not good for the man to be alone; I will make him a helper suitable for him* (Genesis 2:18). The pursuit of a helper was God's effort, not Adam's. There's a garden, there's a man, and then there came God's desire to find the man a helper. God knew it was not good for man to be alone. He knew it because it was the same for Him.

While the picture of the creation of woman differs, the attention and tenderness remain. The Greek word for "made" in Genesis 2:22 can be translated "fashioned." He fashioned the woman. He drew a rib from man and fashioned, in such detail, everything He wanted her to be. We aren't some picture He colored or an over-glorified play-dough creation. We are formed in His image and filled with the same breath that God breathes. The connection God must have desired between the two of us is so great. He wanted us to have a piece of Him inside of us. He wanted us to relate, to bond, to be one.

Am I saying that God was lonely and so He created us? No, well, yes, but no. No in the sense that God is not emotionally needy the way we are. God is God. He is whole, complete and without fault. He could have existed just fine without us; in fact, He did. But He *wanted* us. He wanted our presence, our conversation, our time, and most of all, our love. "Man's need that was satisfied in woman was the same as God's need that was satisfied in creating us."[1] Have you ever allowed yourself to think you were that important? Don't you see how passionately God wants you and I? And for the life of us, we can't figure out why just sitting on our beds and reading a chapter of the Bible isn't cutting it. We were designed for more! And if you are anything like me, you've been settling for less.

God has been courting you for a while. I know this because I watched how He courted me. When I first met God, He was just a friend of my parents.

---

1   Pastor Robert Morris, Gateway Church. Southlake, Texas.

We spent time every week going to His house. We sang songs about Him (some in a language I barely knew), we talked about Him, and we always asked Him to bless our food. I began to see God become a bigger part of my life the more and more I let Him. I discovered He wanted to hear about the friendships that were hurting me. He cared about clubs I wanted to start and a bike I longed to have.

When my parents fought, my Dad showed me how God was a part of that too. In an Egyptian household, everything sounds like a fight. We are *loud*. When I asked my Dad why we are so loud, he said that it is because "we are a passionate people." I liked the idea of being passionate better than being loud. Passion sounds purposeful, and loud is just, well, loud.

I can remember this one particular fight that I witnessed between my parents. It was loud—I mean, passionate. I was afraid. But my Dad pulled me up on his lap and told me that in marriage, you are committed for life. He explained that in our church, when you got married, you made a promise to God that you would stay together through good times and bad. Well, actually, his exact words were, "Americans get divorced, but Coptic Orthodox Egyptians stay together." He explained that even if you fight, you know you are always going to stay together. I learned a lot about the differences between our family and the "American" world that day. But even more so, I learned a lot about God.

Soon, God wasn't just my parents' friend; He

was my friend too. I believe there is a courting into friendship that goes on between you and God. I think we first experience Him as our hero (we call Him "Savior" for that) and then as a Friend.

To say I grew up in church sounds too simple. I grew up in churches. Every Sunday I would hop on the church bus and attend a local church while my parents stayed at home. My parents would listen to the entire three-hour mass on tape while we were gone. There was not a local Coptic Orthodox Church in Alabama (imagine that), so my parents went above and beyond to stay faithful.

Once a month we would drive for four hours to Atlanta to go to the Coptic Orthodox Church that my parents helped start. We would get up really early in the morning on Saturday and return by Sunday afternoon. This was how I grew up, with one foot in the Orthodox world and the other in the Protestant world.

In 1988, when I was eleven, I attended a children's camp. One night, the sermon was on Shadrach, Meshach and Abednego, three men who stood for what they believed in the presence of a king who didn't agree. They were committed, all the way to the furnace. And they weren't alone; Jesus was there with them in the midst of the fire. At the end of the night, we were invited to come forward and ask this same Jesus to stand by us. This was an easy decision for me. It wasn't the first time I had heard of Jesus; I had seen Him in my family already. I was ready. I

Like me, you probably entered into a marriage with your Friend and not with your Lover*.*

wanted Jesus to be by my side. He had courted me to this place and I had no worries about saying yes! I went forward, inviting Him to hang out with me.

But I wanted more.

Is that where you are? Are you craving more? He is inviting you into something beyond your current understanding of Him.

There is a deeper level that can occur between you and God; this one, although it still involves friendship, seeks more intimacy. He wants to be your Husband—your Lover. Now in our world, you don't just put a statement out there like that: "I want to be your lover." Usually there is a more spiritually correct statement, like, "God is the Bridegroom and you are His bride." The word *lover* implies too much. *Husband* says we can still keep a *Leave It To Beaver*-like picture of God. You are together. It is a real commitment. You do things for Him, He does things for you. You live in a beautiful and safe home with a white picket fence, and no one intrudes or disrupts you. It is predictable. It is useful. Did I mention it's safe? And it is common; just look down the pew—there are a lot of marriages like yours.

Like me, you probably entered into a marriage with your Friend and not with your Lover. You live with God, but you are never intimate with Him. You are close with Him. You ask His advice about everything. You go everywhere together. But once you get home—

it's two separate twin beds in the bedroom.

This deeper courtship, the one leading to Him as your Husband, was supposed to include the role of Lover in its description, but it somehow got left out. (That part never gets left out in the beginning of a real marriage, does it?) We know and welcome Him as Friend and Husband, but now God is drawing us even more deeply as lovers.

One of the first signs of His wooing is discontent. Remember that craving for more? I don't know why God thinks that we aren't motivated enough to get ourselves to a better place in our relationship, but obviously He thinks we need some help. Unrest sets in. All of a sudden, you aren't excited anymore about doing the same thing year after year in your relationship with God. You have bought book after book, study after study, and yet the dissatisfaction remains.

Or maybe you've done the Bible roulette game or the Bible-in-a-year (or like me the two or three-year) chart. They weren't bad; you just weren't that different after you were through. And that fact alone breeds dissatisfaction. I am not content with my relationship with God. Is it a dry spell? Do I need a different devotional? Do I need to volunteer more? Is there sin in my life? Maybe. Probably not. Probably so. And most likely yes, so confess it.

But the issue is not your behavior; it's Who is drawing you. He is calling out to you, telling you, "There's more." *What? I didn't just hear that. That's too disruptive. I live in Safeville; you can't say that to me. My life is what everyone dreams about. I do my devotions every day. I donate goods to charity at holidays. I go to church every Sunday, Wednesday, and any other day they tell us to. I go to conferences. I listen to Christian radio. I read Christian books. I only know Christian people. There can't be more! Because to believe there is more is to recognize that I am living with less.*

One moment you were perfectly content, living the life you thought you always wanted, and now you feel lost. Well, if Safeville is not where you want to be, then where are you supposed to go?

A quick word of caution: every new idea that enters your life from this point on is not a message straight from God. First of all, *there is nothing new under the sun* (Ecclesiastes 1:9). If God is trying to say something to you, it will agree with His Word. It has to agree with His Word; He can't go against Himself—that is His nature.

I was in a very safe place with God. Married to my high school sweetheart, working at the church I grew up in, living in my hometown—I was the poster-child for Safeville when the call for more began to stir inside of me. But instead of pressing in, I acted out. Not like a two-year old in a grocery store; I just decided that if I felt God speaking to me, it meant I needed to *do* something. So I did. We did. We picked up our stuff and moved three states west to Texas. I would pursue my PhD, have a baby and maybe even help out in a ministry. As long as I was *doing* for God, I knew everything was right between us. My doing made me feel like I was safe.

Surely uprooting my family and leaving would quiet this feeling. I had *done* a lot for God. But the echo for more could not be silenced. In frustration I cried out to Him, "I am doing all I can! What more can I do to encounter You?"

God was answering me, but I wasn't ready for what He had to say. He was wooing me, drawing me deeper, but I thought that just meant I needed to *do* more. I had the idea of being married to God all wrong. I grew up understanding that a relationship with God was about what you *did* for Him. "He died for you, the least you could do is live for Him." But that wasn't God's bumper sticker; it was man's.

I wanted more, and I began to discover that it had everything to do with *doing less*. Each crumb, each word from a friend, each sermon I heard, every verse He drew me to—they all trailed the same idea: "Stop *doing* for Me and start loving Me—enjoying Me, talking to Me … having a relationship with Me."

Watch for the ideas that keep repeating themselves. "I was just reading this passage in the Bible that the pastor is talking about today. And then I was talking to a friend about a problem I was having and she told me something that was exactly what the pastor had just said on Sunday. And then I picked up a magazine that was talking about the very same thing." There's His voice again. Only this time, it doesn't make

make you panic. It makes you wonder. It makes you think. It makes you feel. You are getting a heart, a brain and courage! By golly, it looks as though you are coming alive inside. You aren't the cookie cutout that the enemy hopes you would remain. You are burning rubber on the road out of Safeville as you begin questioning the things you've always just accepted.

What if there is more? And what if that more is linked to all these things that keep crossing your path?

But God is not the only one trying to woo you. There is another: Satan. Many followers have strayed onto a wide path because of a bad idea.

> *Don't look for shortcuts to God. The market is flooded with surefire, easygoing formulas for a successful life that can be practiced in your spare time. Don't fall for that stuff, even though crowds of people do. The way to life—to God!—is vigorous and requires total attention.*
>
> -Matthew 7:13, MSG

This is your life, your choice; be intentional with it.

Satan would love to court you. Does that surprise you? Is that a fearful statement? It should be a sobering one. Most of us are content with the idea that God is pursuing us, but to think that Satan attempts to as well makes you think differently about your days. Here's the bottom line—courting is ultimately about making a choice. God's ultimate goal is for you to say "yes!" He is on one knee, asking you to see who He is and agree to spend forever with Him. When you say "yes," it is a done deal. Who you are, your identity, is settled: You are His and He is yours. Your value and your worth—settled and settled.

Think about Adam and Eve in the garden. (I know, not our finest moment as humans.) God was calling them into a relationship with Him. He designed the world for them. Every day, they affirmed their "yes" to Him. Then along came Satan. He wanted Adam and Eve's affection, too. So what did he use to woo them? Their identity. Satan told them that if they ate from the tree of the knowledge of good and evil, they would be like God (Genesis 3:5). But wait a minute, they were *already* like God; they had been created in His image (Genesis 1:27).

We don't like the picture of another lover. We don't like to believe he really exists. Well, he exists, we admit, but not intimately—so we think. So I thought. And his methods haven't changed. I thought my identity was settled. I belonged, and yet the enemy tried to convince me that I was spiritually single, isolated—and alone.

Before Kenneth and I moved to Texas, I had a plan. I could tell you what I wanted to do for the next five years. After high school, I knew college was next. After college was seminary, and after seminary was supposed to be my PhD (you already know how that turned out). Each step that I took, each goal achieved,

I began to turn toward the affections of another. Were the things that I was doing wrong? No, but my affections are what the spiritual world wages war over. The enemy knew what he was doing. I began to trade the settled truth of my identity for a lie:

Your value is settled.
with
Your value is earned.

You are already successful.
with
Your success is "to be determined."

Your destiny is now.
with
Your destiny is a moving target.

It isn't the enemy's wooing that creates the problem; it is what I choose to do with that wooing. Do I believe it? Do I let it into my mind, my heart? Most of all, do I lie down with it? I did. Normally, the bedroom doesn't belong in the courting process. But Satan doesn't care. He is hell-bent on destroying me. He will woo me, use me, and then forget my number. I now know what to call what he does: *lying*. I gave permission to Satan by agreeing with a lie. How did I agree with the lie? I thought about the lie, dwelled on the lie, marinated in it until it became a belief. It was easy to see that it was a belief by looking at my actions. I was seeking people to affirm and confirm what God had already affirmed and confirmed in me. Was my preaching deep enough? Was the program organized well? Was the game we played good? Was I funny? Did the kids like me? Did their parents? On and on it would go.

I Peter 5:8 says, *Be self-controlled and alert. Your enemy the devil prowls around like a roaring lion looking for someone to devour* (NIV). He is waiting. There are no actions in life that have a neutral spiritual effect on you. You are walking towards one courter or the other. But here is the difference between the two: one loves you and one hates you. One admits His emotion, while the other conceals it in order to draw you in.

Satan wants the end result of acknowledging his activity to bring fear. I want it to bring perspective that leads to a paradigm shift, making you think. The kind of thinking that changes your beliefs.

I am not asking you to become "the little engine that could." You cannot just think *harder* and thus become better. By myself, I cannot become any better than I already am. That way of thinking is where I lived for most of my relationship with God. When I said "yes" to God, I got to throw off all my old filthy rags and take on Jesus' robes of righteousness. When God sees me, He sees the righteousness of Christ all over me.

You are made up of three parts: your spirit, your soul and your body. When you say "yes" to God, your spirit is entirely and wholly saved, but your soul (your mind, will and emotions) is learning how to adjust to that reality. It was used to being in charge. Now your spirit has taken the lead, and at times your soul does not like it. When you sin, it is you making a choice based on who you *were*, the "old man" (Colossians 3:9), and not who you *are*. You are already a child of God, no longer a slave. You are already rich, no longer impoverished. You are already the bride, no longer just in the bridal party.

How do we change the way our soul operates? We need to examine our beliefs. What we believe determines how we make choices, express our emotions, even how we speak our words. What determines our beliefs? Our identity—who we believe we are—and our thoughts. If we are in Christ, the issue of our identity is already settled. So what we have left to work with is our thoughts. Every day you will have the opportunity to entertain several thoughts, and each one can either strengthen or weaken a belief. II Corinthians 10:5 advises us to *take every thought captive and make it obedient to Christ*. Why do we need to be so aggressive about our thoughts? Because they build up our beliefs, and our beliefs are the sources of our actions.

This takes time. In the past, courtship was a process. Men and women walked and talked together, day after day, making decisions, sharing thoughts and feelings, becoming intimately acquainted with one another. It isn't just one dramatic choice at an altar that keeps you close to God. It is choice after choice, day after day, thought after thought, choosing to be with the one you want to be courted by. Every day, agreeing with *whose* you already are.

So where is He courting you? Where do you feel His hand gently guiding you? Recently, I have experienced God drawing me deeper through an unexpected area of my life: my finances. Sounds romantic, doesn't it? But intimacy is not just about our emotions.

Many times I have wanted God to stay in the box I put Him in, but He longs to move from being just a part of my life to being my *whole* life. Often I keep Him out of areas that I don't want Him to speak into. But I know that I would seriously question the wife who made her husband stay in only one room of the house.

Why do we not give God free access to everything in our lives? Fear. We are afraid of what He will see, we are afraid of what He will say, we are afraid of not being safe any more. But God did not give us a spirit of fear, *but of POWER and LOVE and SOUND MIND* (II Timothy 1:7, emphasis mine).

Fear is not a part of who we are—we are powerful, loved, and wise. God did not promise us safety; ask John the Baptist, who sat in prison waiting for his beheading. Jesus was right there, in the same town, and He did not go and break John out of jail (Luke 7:18-39). We are not promised safety, we are promised peace. Peace that surpasses our understanding, our circumstances, our situations, our questions, and our fears (Philippians 4:7). It doesn't mean we don't have doubts or can't ask God to confirm what He has said to us; even John asked Jesus to confirm who He was. It just means that we cannot look to safety as a marker of peace or intimacy.

One of the ways God courts us into different places of intimacy is through planting an idea. For me, it started simply. I kept reading things about God's power to provide financially, and began praying about this area in my family's life.

I grew up in a middle-class, well-educated family. My dad was a professor for the University of Alabama with two PhDs—one in physics and one in chemistry. My mom is brilliant as well; she received her Masters in education while living in Germany. When they moved to the United States, my dad worked to provide for our family and my mom gave up her goals to stay at home and take care of me and my sister Halla. She took on odd jobs to help make middle-class life work. We were not poor, we were not rich; we landed squarely in the middle.

My first taste of budgeting came when I moved away from Alabama to go to college in Indiana. I had $600 for the entire semester. With no car at school, I had to work that budget for all it was worth. I worked an on-campus job and tried to sell knives on the side. The knives gig didn't work. With no car and no students that I knew able to afford the high-class knives, I was left pinching pennies.

I did discover one way to make my budget stretch.

When I would go home, about one or two times a semester, I would inevitably be taken to Wal-Mart to restock. I loved this trip to Wal-Mart. I would stock up on everything I needed—and didn't need. That's right, *didn't need*. I would buy razors, even if I didn't need them. "Why?" you ask? Because I was brilliant. I would take my items back to school with me, load up my shelves and wait. There would come a time when I needed money—and now I had a solution: I would just take some items back to Wal-Mart and return them. In those days, they gave you cash back for your returned items. I may have single-handedly been the cause for Wal-Mart putting tighter restrictions on their return policies.

I knew how to get what I wanted. I don't think that means I knew how to budget my money, even though I thought it did.

So without being aware of my past financial life affecting my future one, I got married. I carried my middle-class "I can make this work" mentality into our finances as well. Together, we started a new chapter, but with the same theme—to make ends meet. With each paycheck earned, our bills skimmed it away. With each increase, our "needs" changed. We eventually discovered that our true need was change.

Now, as I felt the Lord courting me, I wanted to be released from the burden of making ends meet. But once I opened the door to that thought, a flood came with it. I began to realize how mixed up my wants and needs had become. I was putting a "needs" label on everything. I would be in the grocery store (a horrible place to decipher between needs and wants), trying to check items off my list, and God would speak right there.

"Do you need that?"

"It's Wal-Mart, God. I need everything."

But I knew what He meant. I didn't have to try every new thing that was advertised. I didn't have to have the latest or greatest items on display. I needed to allow Him to court me into a new thought: I could say no and the world would not end. I could still have a good day. Days later, God would show me how I was looking to my own means to provide and not to Him. I was always looking for Kenneth's pay to increase, or a side job I could do to bring in some more money; all ways in which to balance my steadily rising list of "needs." Then He would challenge me again: had I prayed before I bought that or paid that bill? Did I truly believe that God would want to court me in this area after we had failed in it so many times? Wouldn't my past financial failures cause Him to look for someone else? Each thought drew me closer and closer to the One that so desperately wanted to be all that I needed, financially and more.

That thought, that impulse, that reminder ... it wasn't from me. My husband and I laugh at the names we gave the Holy Spirit before we had a relationship with Him. My name for Him was "crazy." Kenneth's name for Him was "something."

"That is so 'crazy' that my friend called, I was just

thinking about her today."

"I don't know what it is, but 'something' is telling me that I don't need to pursue this deal."

The Holy Spirit is the one whom Jesus sent after He left. In fact, He told us it is better for us to have the Holy Spirit than for Him to remain. Jesus walked with the people, but the Holy Spirit lives inside of us. We all know that *inside* is closer than *beside*. Intimacy occurs not because we let God into *part* of our lives, but into all of it—every aspect.

Maybe your courtship is starting in something practical like finances. Or it could occur in places like your dreams. Could it be through your parenting or your position? Once you have given permission to the idea that God can be your Husband, it isn't a question of *if* He will court you, it's how.

You can flip the page and go on reading the next chapter in order to hurry up and finish another book. Or you can stop the pace of this hurried life and really think about the question God is asking. Is He pursuing you as a friend? Is He drawing you into marriage? Is He wooing you as His lover? One is not better than the other; it's not like climbing rungs on a ladder. But no one was meant to court forever; eventually a commitment is made … another response is required.

chapter three | **battle**

Two sides and only one can win—a battle, your battle. God wants to be close to us. But as we've seen, there is someone else who would love to keep Him far away: Satan. Our hearts are the battlefield, and this battle is too critical for either side to lose.

I have contributed many times to God losing this battle in my life. Sometimes I'd think I had gained some ground in this area, only to find it was a hollow victory. But that's what I love about God: He takes my false encounters with intimacy and redeems them. He doesn't give me something that is just good enough, though. He gives me His best, His plan A, custom-fit for me. Let me show you what my battle looked like; maybe it will help you on your own journey. And then we'll figure out how to help you fight.

I can't say that I was scared of intimacy. I was actually too fond of it—at least what I thought was intimacy. I searched for it in the wildest and darkest of places.

I grew up in your average white suburban community. Remember now, I'm Egyptian. I accounted for possibly the lowest minority representation ever in an elementary school. I knew of around ten African-Americans, a couple of Chinese kids and maybe some children from India. I wish God had looked down at me then and said, "It is not good for Irini to be alone," and placed the coolest person in school beside me to be my very best friend. It didn't happen.

I felt very alone. My mother only helped in this separation between me and what I called normal: she cut my hair for me. My hair is naturally curly, but when cut in a bowl shape it is naturally poofy; sort of like an Afro, but not as cool. My clothes were never the appropriate length as I was tall and long jeans had yet to be invented. My dad contributed to our oddness by painting our house in suburbia an "oops" color of green. It was like the signs in Las Vegas, all lit up shouting, "Hey, we're foreign!" All I wanted at the time was to be white, blonde and from a normal divorced family.

I longed for a real relationship. I battled for it in my thoughts, in my feelings, in my words. I sought friendships that returned void. Not that they weren't my "friends," but they were one-sided friendships. I would do anything for them … but oops, none for you, Irini. I realized very early on that intimacy cannot be forced; it either exists or it does not. If only one desires it, then you have a stalker on your hands. I began to realize that true friendship was much more than what I could give people in order for them to give me something in return.

There are intimate acts, and then there is the state of being *intimate*. The acts are all the things we do to gain intimacy. Think about some common ways in which we go about becoming closer to God. If I had to think back to my childhood—elementary, junior high, even high school, college, through my masters, at times even now—works, or earning my way, was the common thread through all these years. It saddens me that I just recently got over feeling guilty if I didn't do my devotions for the day.

What I believed was that if I wanted to be closer to God, I should do more for Him. Now, don't get me wrong; I agree that *faith without works is dead* (James 2:26). But faith is first in line in that scripture. You cannot have faith without having a relationship, but you can have a relationship without faith. The first relationship gives you the assurance and the certainty to move and grow in ways that you could never think, dream or imagine. The second relationship is draining and leads nowhere. I lived a lot of my life thinking that what I did for God determined how close I could be with Him.

But the state of *being* intimate goes far beyond actions. In a real relationship, if it were soley about actions, it would never work. Think about a close relationship you have: friend, spouse, family member, etc. Now what if I told you that the only way to get closer to them was if you did something for them?

There are intimate acts, and then there is being intimate.

Even if it were nice things like feed the homeless, give to the needy, or raise money for a cure, at some point, you would become frustrated. At some point, you would say, "Why is it not enough to just be with me?"

This is where I felt trapped. I wanted more than just a relationship based on works. I craved a relationship that involved me and God and no one else. I didn't want random acts of intimacy, where one day I would be close to God because I did something right and then the next day was "to be determined." I wanted the *state* of intimacy—the confident place that says that no matter what I do, I can still be close to Him. I was engaged in a battle between *acting* intimate and the state of *being* intimate.

My battle to conquer intimacy continued into junior high. This was different territory for me, because at the age of eleven, I had entered into a relationship with God. It sounds so corny to say it that way, as though I just stepped into a room or arrived at a destination. But God and I hooked up, and now I had found a partner in crime. He would help me find true friends. (It's that sort of junior-high logic that reinforces why Jesus needs to come back before my children go to junior high.)

I wasn't seeking for God to be my source; more like I wanted Him to be Santa Claus. If I desired a friend—poof, I would get one under my tree at my home in Woodland Forrest. A boyfriend? There he would stand, at the best party of the year. (Wait; maybe that's not just junior-high logic after all. I still catch myself thinking that way.) Sure, I had friends, mainly because I convinced my parents to let me have two parties where my older sister was the only one in charge.

The first party was good, but the second party was great. At the second party, I was set up. My sister, being older and cooler, knew one of the boys at the party. She asked him to dance with me. I thought, "Yes, Santa, you are coming to town!" Finally, I would get what I had wanted for so long: a guy would like me. We danced that awkward junior high dance, but inside, I thought I had arrived. This party would be the climax thus far in my life—a first boyfriend and eventually, at another party, a kiss. It was a vague form of intimacy and I had what I thought I wanted, yet I was still unfulfilled. So I stopped the parties, which disbanded my "loyal" friends, and the boyfriend quickly disappeared because his mother thought I was a bad influence due to my notorious parties. My last year of junior high was very lonely.

I found friendships in the church, but even there I found that everything was contingent upon my spiritual performance. "If you behave right and you bring friends, we like you." I am very good at figuring out what others like in order to please them. And pleasing them was the link to a real relationship, right? Well, at least that was what I thought. In actuality, that is how I formed my thoughts about God as well. *Do*, and you will receive His approval. If this is what the church said, it must be the echo of God. I was in choir, drama team, leadership, the youth band ... you name it, and I was in it, *doing* for God.

Church wasn't the only place I learned some new tools. I found a new set of friends on my track team in high school as well. These ladies were the "experienced ones," having intimacy down pat in an area I had never really explored. We used to call each other by numbers on the team: the numbers stood for how many times you had been with a guy. Other girls' numbers soared while mine sat at a nice fat zero. My requirements at church were coming into conflict with my requirements on the track team. Here were ladies reaching the heights of what I thought was intimacy and I was left to struggle with who was right. So I decided to strike a balance between the two. I would remain faithful to the church while exploring physical intimacies to new levels—but never crossing the ever-forbidden SEX LINE. Now I could try my hand at both.

This awakened a whole new need in me. I liked physical intimacy. I liked someone looking at me and saying I was beautiful. I needed someone to approve of my looks, my smile, my likes and dislikes in a way no one ever had before. I wanted more than someone who would say, "Yeah, that's my friend." I wanted someone who would look me up and down and say, "WOW, I *like* her." Our wants are a very dangerous breeding ground, and I began to rank this need higher than mere friendship. For it seemed that if I was intimate physically, I got the physical touch, the affirming words and the bonus of a cool friend to talk on the phone with every night.

I wanted this so desperately in high school. What was left so unfulfilled in me that I hungered after it this way? My father loved me and told me that he loved me. I had achieved the milestone of having a boyfriend. I even had a handy friend named Jesus with me. Back and forth the battle raged.

But I had not settled who I was. Although I knew in my head Christ died on the cross for me, I didn't agree with that truth in my heart and let it become something I believed. I had no idea what that meant about who I was, how valuable that made me. So every time my boyfriend said I looked good, every time he kissed me, held my hand or put his arm around me, I felt affirmed about who I was—or who I thought I was. This thing, this need, was like a black hole: it had no end. I always wanted more.

As much as I liked the attention I got from a boyfriend I was physical with, my heart was still aching for something else. I knew I needed more. I felt guilty all the time because I was disappointing someone while pleasing another. Church and boyfriends can be a hard mix.

I decided to confess my struggle to a leader in the church. Although they seemed to listen, all I heard from them was, "You'd better get your act straight or you will be kicked out of leadership." I loved leadership; I got the attention of people, which was as good as any relationship for me. People approved of me, and I equated that to being one rung closer to God. On the other hand, I loved my boyfriend; I got his attention, which, again, was one of the best things that I knew. My boyfriend liked me and thus I got to climb another rung.

I felt caught.

To maintain one relationship caused the other that I loved to become threatened. I wanted both. The truth is that I really didn't know what I wanted—not yet, at least. But while true intimacy can be gained from understanding your value, you cannot find your value in intimacy; at least, not a worldly intimacy. Your value is not a variable; it's a fact. It doesn't fluctuate or change with the relationships or circumstances around you.

The lesson I learned was that human intimacy would fail me, and so I just kept my forbidden behavior in the dark. But it's hard to see when it's dark. And if you don't know where you're going or what you're pursuing, you can end up in the loneliest and most difficult places.

I escaped my physical struggle only because I graduated and went to college. Now I was in the realm of what I thought was "grown up": I tried a new ladder to climb into the *Holy of Holies*—through intellect. I had a boyfriend that was different from all my other boyfriends. I really wasn't attracted to him physically. Even holding his hand made me feel weird—but I loved talking to him. We would go to a coffee shop in Marion, Indiana and talk all night. We would read poetry to each other; not the mushy love ones, but poems about God. Afterwards, we would talk about who God is and where we were headed after college. What I liked about this relationship was that it had nothing to do with how I looked—the color of my skin, what I wore, or even if my hair was behaving that day. This guy cared about what I *thought*. It was refreshingly different. I had never known intimacy like this. Our minds truly connected, and my standards rose. I knew that when I finally experienced true intimacy, this would have to be one aspect of it.

What I failed to realize was that God put that craving within me. When He took the risk of giving me free will, He carved a need in me for intimacy to lead me back to Him. He knew I would fail; He knew I would look in other places to try and fill my need. But He also knew that if I searched, I would find my fulfillment in Him. My craving is, in a way, God's safety net for the risk of free will.

The battle is hard. I say *is* hard, because it is still a battle for me. I recognize now that God is the truest source of intimacy, but that doesn't keep me from seeking it in the wrong places sometimes. As I battled, I created addictions: addictions to what people thought of me; or performance, even using physical intimacies to secure it.

Doug Bannister in his book *Sacred Quest* writes

about the idea that we seek people to fill our voids.[2] If we are not fulfilled by our intimacies with God then we will walk into every relationship requiring a toll payment: "Fill my void." I found myself doing this early on in my marriage. I was asking Kenneth to be what only God could be in my life.

I love to talk. (You are surprised, I know.) Once, when asked to make up a story to keep my pastor entertained on a road trip, arriving at our destination was the only reason the story ended. So you can imagine that words and time are my big love languages—how I like for love to be spoken to me. Now, it would be highly convenient if Kenneth's love language was also words and time. If you are married, you're probably already shaking your head. And you would be right. Imagine that, a married couple with differences. I now think that that could be part of the definition of marriage: differences. But when I first married Kenneth, I thought that the fact that we were different meant something was wrong with us.

So I wanted to turn Kenneth into a mini-me. I wanted him to like to talk for hours about deep and senseless things. I wanted him to stay up as our heads hit the pillow at night—when I began to talk. To be honest, I think I was one step away from painting his nails.

When Kenneth wouldn't respond like I wanted him to, it hurt. But the truth that I discovered was that

---

2   Bannister, Doug. *Sacred Quest*. Grand Rapids: Zondervan, 2001. Print.

unless I handed him a daily script to follow, he wasn't going to meet my pre-conceived expectations every time we talked. But I know someone who knows my thoughts better than I do, who has figured out my emotions even better than I can. And when I lay my head down at night, He even likes to talk to my spirit in my dreams. He loves to talk to me. Every chance I give Him, He speaks. Kenneth can affirm the things that God fulfills—but not be the fulfiller. If I am not careful, I will enter into friendships, work relationships and even those I counsel with a need for them to meet my needs.

One struggle has been with my destiny. Many people have spoken greatness into my life, and I have always been marked as "different." Being told that God was going to do some extraordinary things in my life created hope; hope is alluring—so I discovered.

I am so grateful for those who have spoken into my life. But if other people are the only place I hear from my Husband, there is a problem. He longs to speak to me directly. It is God showing how extravagant His love is when He repeats His message through others.

Instead of tracing my hope to God, I marked my own path, straight to my destiny. It started with a dependence on words of encouragement, of wisdom, even prophetic words. I sought others to affirm what I sensed in my heart. But why didn't I go directly to my Husband and talk to Him? Didn't I believe that *I* could hear from God? Didn't I believe *what* I had already heard from God? Where the battle raged the hardest was during the silent times. The enemy would speak his own words to me, and he had much to say about my past, my inadequacies, my failures, and more.

"You are a just a woman. Ministry is for men."

"You are too young. Just wait until you have more experience."

"They may like you now, but what if they knew about your past?"

What Satan tried to damage was my identity. He was very convincing.

When we moved from Alabama to Texas, I discovered a disheartening silence. No kids, no parents, no bosses, no professors, no mentors, no colleagues, no friends—nothing. It was just Kenneth and me. It felt the same in the spiritual—it was just God and me. Kenneth and I had a lot of tournaments on our Pac-Man machine that first year. You spend more time with your Husband when there are no other options. But what started as the words of others has grown into something greater: a word directly from God. It took moving away from all those voices to hear the voice of my Husband.

And now, here's what I'm going to do: I'm going to start all over again. I'm taking her back out into the wilderness where we had our first date, and I'll court her.

-Hosea 2:14, MSG

That is what Texas was, my wilderness. But just like in Hosea, it became the place that God courted me deeply and battled for me fiercely. I discovered that God was for me. That He was jealous for me and my affections. I believe God has called me to greatness, not at the exclusion of others, but at the inclusion of them.[3] A greatness that means I am achieving what God had destined for me; a greatness that draws that out in others too. But now I fear I am having a love affair with my destiny. I think about it, I pray about it, I talk to people about it. I am obsessed with it as if it is the key to my approval and thus to my ultimate fulfillment.

But don't I know by now that my relationship with God is about who I am and not what I do? I did nothing to gain His love and therefore I can do nothing to keep it. I understand that, but am I okay with it? It's okay with me that I am not exactly where I want to be right now, because greatness is in my future. One day I will be where I want to be. But what if something changes? Have I created a new belief to replace the old? If all my works and efforts are removed, what am I left with?

Do you hear the rhythms of the battle?

Who I am right now, who He is—that's what remains. The intimacy I experience today is greater than what I have experienced in the past, but it is far

---

3   Henri Nouwen

more real and tangible than what I can only imagine will come in the future. I am not saying that I shouldn't hope for more in my intimacy with God; otherwise, why write this book? But I am saying that my hope for the future shouldn't diminish the pleasure of my present intimacy.

For some, your battle has not been with people or things replacing God, but with intimacy itself. You hear the word "intimacy" and immediately, it strikes fear within you. All of your experiences with it have been negative. Maybe it was from a parental relationship, an abusive experience, a friendship gone awry, a marriage that isn't working the way you thought it would; you fill in the blank. All you know is that a distant God is more appealing than a close one. Is God's presence in our lives bringing forth the emotions we feel in front of a cop, or with a lover?

Unhealthy fear is a tool of Satan, but there are healthy fears. The fear of falling when you are looking over a cliff is healthy because it makes you stay a safe distance from the edge. The fear of losing control of your car if you drive too fast—again, healthy, because it makes you drive more slowly (well, some of us). And yes, healthy fears can turn unhealthy when taken to the extremes, but most things taken to the extremes are unhealthy, even godly things. So how do we battle this fear of intimacy? How do we confront it and defeat it?

Some of you cringe at the thought. You have run

from it and continue to run. You know it when you see it and have stayed far from it. But whatever place you land on the spectrum, one thing is for certain: the battle is still waging. While you may think your struggle is wrapped up in a boyfriend, spouse, job or family, it's not! The battle is so much bigger.

For our struggle is not against flesh and blood, but against the rulers, against the powers, against the world forces of this darkness, against the spiritual forces of wickedness in the heavenly places.
-Ephesians 6:12

There is a battle going on every day, and it isn't with the lady behind the checkout counter or the car in front of you when you are late. The battle goes on in the spiritual realm. That may sound weird to you, like something from a sci-fi movie or a really poorly made Christian movie. But that is part of what Satan would have us believe—the notion that all there is to life is what we can see. Oh, but there is so much more. Satan has his army, but God has angels fighting on your behalf too. And our prayers, our thoughts, our beliefs, our actions and our habits can help or hurt the battle for us.

So what are the tools that God has given us to battle with—and win—in the arenas of intimacy?

Therefore put on the full armor of God, so

that when the day of evil comes, you may be able to stand your ground, and after you have done everything, to stand. Stand firm then, with the belt of truth buckled around your waist, with the breastplate of righteousness in place, and with your feet fitted with the readiness that comes from the gospel of peace. In addition to all this, take up the shield of faith, with which you can extinguish all the flaming arrows of the evil one. Take the helmet of salvation and the sword of the Spirit, which is the word of God.

-Ephesians 6:13-17

Sounds basic, right? You expected something a little more complex or edgy, something you had never thought about before. But remember, there is no "God's Word, part II." Everything we need has already been given to us. I often forget to apply the basics of my faith, because I am in pursuit of something new, unheard of, or cutting-edge. That's a trap too. (Maybe it's even false intimacy.) So what do we do with these tools that God has given us?

Think of an area where you are battling right now. What is fighting for your passion, your thoughts, your time, your money and your dreams? Let's generically pick ... people. (Okay, it's not generic. I love people and trying to please them is hard not to do. But I already confessed that to you.)

So let's go with that example.

> You are a person (deep thought, I know).
>
> You were designed with a need for intimacy.
>
> You were a kid once.
>
> As a kid, you were affirmed when you did something right.
>
> You liked how that affirmation made you feel.
>
> You felt close to the person that affirmed you.
>
> As a result, you linked affirmation with intimacy.

Sounds harmless, until I grew up—I mean, until this hypothetical person grew up.

> Now, you are still a person (still deep, I know).
>
> You are still designed with a need for intimacy.
>
> You are an adult now (theoretically).
>
> You receive affirmation.
>
> You like how that affirmation makes you feel.
>
> As a result, you want that affirmation to continue.
>
> You think that affirmation fulfills the need for intimacy.
>
> Actually, you think that people, the ones who affirm you, fulfill that need for intimacy.

You look to people to affirm you, so that you feel valued.

As a result, you allow people to determine your value.

So how does the armor of God help us in the battle? Let's begin with the first piece of armor the scripture begins with: *the belt of truth* (v. 14a). On its most basic level, a belt gives you confidence. Not in form but in function: a belt helps you keep your pants on. Or for a Roman soldier, that cute little battle skirt with the leather strips. While he might have hated the skirt, the soldier must have been thankful for the belt that held it up. That is what truth does for us in our lives, in our battles—it gives us confidence.

Whatever it is that you battle, the first front of attack is truth. Ask yourself: *What is true about the thought I just had? What is true about the emotion I just felt? What is true about what that person just said? What is true about people determining my value?* While reciting the truth can seem like a thoughtless activity, it isn't. You may hate the truth, but that doesn't change it. Truth is absolute, and there is power in it.

Believe it or not, our words are powerful. They speak life or death, blessings or curses (Proverbs 18:21). Truth fights against the lies Satan has enticed us with. Many times, we get caught up in our circumstances, all because we believed a lie. We believed that we weren't good enough. We believed that it was okay to be angry and lash out. We believed that we wouldn't amount to anything. We believed that people could determine our value. The only thing that stops a lie is the truth. The truth is that people don't determine our value, God does. He determined it when He chose to create us, and there is nothing anyone can say or anything we can do that can change our value.

Truth can be a thought that enters your mind, but sometimes quickly exits. What has to happen is that you dwell on, think on, marinate in that truth until it becomes a belief in your heart. Truth needs to move past being an accessory to your spiritual wardrobe and become more like a functional necessity. Because after it becomes a belief, it will change your actions. And action upon action creates a habit.

Truth can be both instantaneous and progressive. When we encounter it, we have a choice: to agree with it or reject it, and then to choose that truth every day thereafter. Every thought is an opportunity to strengthen or weaken the truth you have allowed to enter your mind and thus your beliefs. But the battle drums are still beating; the enemy would love to rob you of that truth, one lie at a time. Satan would love to take the freedom that truth has brought to your life; he longs to keep you in bondage. If you are tied up in lies, you are no harm to him. But remember, *when the enemy comes in like a flood, the Spirit of the Lord will raise up a standard against him* (Isaiah 59:19). What is that standard? The truth. Go back to it. Dwell on it, think on it, marinate in what He has spoken to you until it becomes a belief in your heart.

Next comes the *breastplate of righteousness* (v. 14b). Let me take a moment and briefly explain righteousness. Righteousness is to be *made right*. That assumes something is wrong. But this righteousness is not your righteousness, not you making things "right." If you were "right" enough, you wouldn't need this piece of armor. But we aren't right. You're not right, I'm not right. I know it hurts to read it, but it's true. Being good is not the same as righteousness.

It's His righteousness, through Christ. It's a piece of armor that God is giving you to fight a spiritual battle, to protect your heart. You know, the thing your emotions stem from: your core beliefs. *Above all else, guard your heart, for it is the wellspring of life* (Proverbs 4:23, NIV). The only thing that guards your heart is the right thing Christ did for you, paying the debt, giving you His righteousness. All the good things, the "right" things, you have done in your life are not enough to protect you. Satan wants you to think that if you do more good things than bad that you are safe. You will be deemed a good person, and that's good enough. But believing that lie means that you are trading God's metal, proven, guaranteed armor for a t-shirt. Your protective breastplate has been removed and your heart (your emotions and beliefs) is left unguarded.

By Christ dying on the cross, we are no longer slaves to our emotions. We are free. Our thoughts and emotions do not take us captive; we "take them captive and make them obedient to Christ" (II Corinthians 10:5, paraphrase mine). Do you see how battling against the things that try and replace our intimacy with God will bring you closer to Him? Fighting alongside Him draws you closer; fighting against Him pushes you away.

Put *the gospel of peace* (v. 15) on your feet. That might not make sense until you break it down. We think we understand peace: we see it waved on signs, signaled by two fingers in pictures, and mass-marketed during holidays. But the peace we see here is different. God's peace goes *beyond our understanding* (Philippians 4:7). The odd thing is that in this battle, we are advised not to use our feet to run and confront, but to *stand firm* (v. 11). Don't move, and have a peace about that stance. It seems to follow the Psalm 46:10 logic: *Be still, and know that I am God.*

There is a peace in knowing who can always win any battle we face. But you have to have your feet fitted with a readiness that comes from peace. It means that you've thought it, prepared for it, before the battle. You've *been* ready. Almost as if to say, "I've been training for this day my whole life." You know what that readiness feels like; it's a readiness you can comfortably walk in. In the midst of the battle is not the time to find out your shoes are too small; you need the right size God designed just for you.

Readiness comes from a peace that says, "I may

not know how this battle will be won, but I know it will be." A peace that says, "I may not be as close as I want to be with God, but I know His love remains." A peace that says, "Where I am, as crazy as it appears, is where I am supposed to be."

Satan does not know what to do against that kind of peace. He tries to throw anxiety, fear, harder circumstances, confusion and lies at it, but it just won't move us. We are already ready for those attacks. So when Satan tries to tempt us with looking to people to fulfill our needs, we are ready. We know that only God fulfills us, and knowing that brings a peace. We can stop looking around. We can stop being anxious, wondering if this next venture will be fulfilling; we know it can't, so we can stop trying now!

Peace. It lets you be still, enables you to cease striving and let God be God, meeting all of your needs.

In addition to those pieces comes the *shield of faith* (v. 16). As opposed to the belt, breastplate and shoes, this piece is moveable. What makes up our faith is a constant, like the metal shield itself. But its position of protection is always changing, moving to where we need it most during the battle. And just like shields got better and better in their ability to protect the soldier—they were made out of stronger metals, handles were adjusted for comfort, changing the thickness of the metals used, on and on they evolved—our faith grows and changes the longer we are in relationship with Him.

Our faith can only help us, however, if it is placed in the right person. Faith is what we believe can happen even when we can't see it. How can you have a relationship with a God you can't touch? *Faith.* If your faith is in Him, then when something tries to replace Him as your shield, you notice immediately: it would be as if you'd held up a sheet of poster board versus a shield to protect you. Faith is what *extinguishes the flaming arrows of the evil one* (Ephesians 6:16). That means Satan is throwing everything he has at you, but your belief in a God that wants an intimate relationship with you will cause his arrows to fizzle out. Faith says I believe there is someone bigger, someone deeper, someone greater to fulfill my needs.

The *helmet of salvation* (v. 17) is more than an outdated safety precaution; it is the piece that protects your mind. In the heat of battle, the enemy will try using any thought or perception he can to change your core beliefs. Because remember: your thoughts affect your beliefs, your actions; and your actions, when continued, turn into habits. If Satan can get inside your head, he can get inside your heart.

Our salvation saves us from that intrusion. When Jesus died on the cross, He enabled us to be free from the enslavement Satan demands of us. When we enter into a relationship with God through belief in His Son and confession of our sins, we have established our salvation. We know He saved us. We know we have freedom. We know our old person is no longer alive.

But Satan tries to convince us that all of those truths are a lie. He could be trying to convince you that you have to work for it, be a Christian long enough or do enough good things. Maybe he is trying to tell you that there is no way salvation is that easy. His deception skills are honed; he knows what will make you question God. Even though the truth still remains that you are saved, free, dead to your old self and in relationship with Him, perhaps Satan has you believing it's not true. You need to protect your mind, but you are trying to fight with no helmet. That is what Paul is talking about in II Corinthians 10:5: *We demolish arguments and every pretension that sets itself up against the knowledge of God, and we take captive every thought to make it obedient to Christ.* So when we look to others to fill our void, our helmet of salvation reminds us that there is only one who meets all of our needs: God.

And last of all comes the *sword of the Spirit, which is the word of God* (v. 17b). This is the tool that we seem to know the most about, but are most often unprepared to utilize. It is the only offensive weapon God gives us; the rest are defensive.

For many of us, God's Word has become more of a diet than a feast. We take as little as we can so we can say we have read it; you know, so we feel better about ourselves. But is it real? Is His Word really affecting your life? When you struggle with allowing others to determine your value, do you know how to fight that thought with your sword? Before Jesus did any miracles, before He died on the cross, before He rose from the grave, God told Him He loved Him. His value was not in what He did, but in who He was—His Son (Mark 1:9-11). That's a truth for you and I, a tool that we can fight Satan with when we are tempted with the need to impress others so that we feel valued.

The Bible was not designed for duty. It's more like an email or a letter from our Lover. It's the story of who we are, whose we are, and how we fit into the story. His Word will help you fight whatever battle you face.

But how can you use His words to fight if you have never read them? The middle of the battle is not the time to go searching for your sword. You need your sword in hand, with a firm grip. You can fight the enemy's lies with your own words, but there is no power behind them. You did not defeat Satan, God did; only His words carry the power to defeat.

Sure, you can do a search in the middle of a battle to find out what God's Word says about a particular area. But wouldn't it be better if you had taken the time to read, meditate and dwell on His Word beforehand? Wouldn't it be nice to know the words to fight Satan with as soon as the tempting thought comes your way? That's what is so amazing about the Holy Spirit: He can bring back to your mind the things that you have taken time to dwell on—if you've taken that time.

I say *dwell* on God's Word, because we have

gotten too good at reading. We read for speed, we read for acquisition of data, we read for our pleasure. If God's Word is ever going to be a tool that we readily use to fight our spiritual battles, we have to actually spend quality time in it.

Think about these words from *The Message*, II Corinthians 10:3-6:

The world is unprincipled. It's dog-eat-dog out there! The world doesn't fight fair. But we don't live or fight our battles that way— never have and never will. The tools of our trade aren't for marketing or manipulation, but they are for demolishing that entire massively corruptive culture. We use our powerful God-tools for smashing warped philosophies, tearing down barriers erected against the truth of God, fitting every loose thought and emotion and impulse into the structure of life shaped by Christ. Our tools are ready at hand for clearing the ground of every obstruction and building lives of obedience into maturity.

Intimacy is a battle. A battle God has already won for us.

chapter four | **wedding**

If thrones, crowns and a belly dancer are what come to mind when you think of a wedding, then you would have felt right at home at mine. You either like weddings or you don't. They either get you excited, or they are an annoyance to your social calendar (what's left of it anyway). If the latter is the case, my wedding would have sent you spinning.

Kenneth and I were married in the Coptic Orthodox Church. *Pause.* I am waiting for you to make a connection with that statement. For most people, there is none; for others, the closest they come is to picturing scenes from *My Big Fat Greek Wedding.* You would be very close if that movie came to mind, the only difference is that mine was real. (The skinned lamb? He was at my cousin's wedding.)

Weddings in the Orthodox Church are more like a marathon than a sprint. You could show up an hour late to an Orthodox ceremony and still be considered on time. At the front, there are two thrones for the bride and bridegroom to sit in; these feature prominently throughout the ceremony. No, really. Thrones.

Unlike weddings in America, an Orthodox wedding begins at the back. The bride comes to the church in a car; her father will open the door and walk her to the back of the church, where he will hand her to the groom. Together, with the father's blessing, the bride and groom walk down the aisle.

Then comes the procession of the priests and deacons, following in one very vocal accord. During the service, crowns are placed on the couples' heads and robes on their shoulders as the church blesses them, entering into the institution of marriage. (Can you sense the depth and purpose behind each element of the service? It really is beautiful.)

But there is one thing that stands out of place in the whole service. It is a cry. Yes, a cry: a celebration cry that an Egyptian woman sounds at her own will any time during the whole wedding day. Remember, we are a "passionate" people; this is no quiet cry. Try yelling, "Woo!" at the top of your lungs while simultaneously wiggling your tongue back and forth. Be sure to start at a lower pitch and end climaxing at a much higher pitch. One thing is for sure: you are never prepared for it.

And since we are on the topic of things you wouldn't be prepared for, I would have to add the belly dancer. At our wedding, she was a "gift" to us. (We were just thankful that she was different than the one from our engagement—that one was more like an "aspiring belly dancer.") I must clarify that she does not show up at the ceremony; that's a treat for the reception. It's inspiring.

But in the ceremony, once you move past the symbols, the cry, even my bridal party standing for close to two hours by my enthroned side, you will find my favorite part of the whole service: the end. Not because we were finally married, although I loved that fact too; but because of what we did first. In our church, the first thing you do when you are officially married is not to kiss the bride, and it is not to be announced for the first time as husband and wife, it is to bow before the altar in the church. For us, it was an outward symbol of an inward truth: we wanted God to be first in our life together.

So while this might not be what comes to mind when you think of a wedding, your reaction still gives me a glimpse into your mind. Didn't think you were being that vulnerable, did you?

Our reactions, thoughts and words about something reveal a piece of our mind. We all have mental dictionaries. We take this dictionary with us wherever we go, and it cannot be left behind or forgotten. If we are confused or uncertain, it is there for us to refer to. Experiences, education and people who have influenced us help define the words that fill its imaginary pages. And so we stroll into church, into conversations and into books with our minds wrapped around our own way of thinking, understanding and defining.

Later I passed by, and when I looked at you and saw that you were old enough for love, I spread the corner of my garment over you and covered your nakedness. I gave you my solemn oath and entered into a covenant with you, declares the Sovereign Lord, and you became mine.

-Ezekiel 16:8, NIV

Where did your mental dictionary take you with that verse?

'Return faithless people,' declares the Lord, 'for I am your husband.'

-Jeremiah 3:14, NIV

What about that one?

God's Word mentions that we are the bride and He is the bridegroom. Instantly, the nice and tidy package of the flowers and rings (and unfortunately, the chicken dance) appear on the pages of our minds.

It's easier for women to grasp this picture of being "the bride" than it is for men. For both of us, it's hard to see how that can be a reality in our lives. We can handle Him as Savior, Lord, even Friend, but "Husband" is a stretch. We want to understand the dichotomy between what God says and everything we have been taught about Him, so we conveniently make the picture of marriage understandable for ourselves: God's in a tux, I'm in a gown. We walk down an aisle, and we say some words to Him. Flash—we think of ourselves as married and capture that picture in our dictionaries. We are comfortable with that definition, so it stays in the pages of our mind.

Do you think we might have limited this analogy too soon? Have you ever wondered if there was more to this? When you get past the image of the bride and groom, does it ever make you wonder about the bedroom? *That statement is uncomfortable. To think of me and God in the bedroom is going too far.* Comfort meets uncomfortable definition—who will win? We want to reason it away. We need to do something with it so that we can be comfortable again.

There is a discomfort that God allows in our lives, and like anything uncomfortable, we seek ways to get out of the feeling. God's hope is that the exit you choose will draw you closer to Him. Any other way will draw you far from Him. So what if the way to be closer to God is by thinking of your relationship differently?

While we have heard about the bride and groom analogy, most of us have never applied it to our lives. If we truly thought of ourselves as married to God, it would change so many things about our relationship with Him. We have been quick to take His name ("Yes, I am a Christian"), but slow to enter the bedroom.

If we're married to God, why do we still talk and spend time with Him in such a formal manner? It's like we have left God in His tux and we're still in a

It's like we have left God in His tux and we're still in a gown.

gown. We pray stiffly, we ritualistically talk to Him on Sundays, we wake up and do the same thing every morning, "spending time" with Him. Is it a relationship, or a cult? Do I have a choice? How do my personality, desires and gender affect my relationship with Him?

When does a newly married couple change out of their tux and gown? How long do you think it takes them to get those formal clothes off? Days? Weeks? Months? Years? For me, try minutes. Shocking, I know. No one can wait to get out of those formal outfits. As beautiful as they look, they aren't the most comfortable. Besides, everyone knows what happens once the formal clothes come off.

What about God and me? Isn't there an intimacy I am missing by staying so formal with Him? Wait a minute; shouldn't there be some formalized waiting period before I can become intimate with the Most High Being? Shouldn't someone counsel me through intimacies of the unknown? I mean, one wouldn't expect a newcomer to become intimate with God only minutes after their ceremonial union, would they?

Why not? Why do we think a person has to become cultured in our Christian ways before we allow them to experience the true intimacies of God? I believe that new believers experience intimacy with God more frequently than old believers do. Why? Probability. The more you're in the bedroom, the higher the chances intimacy will happen. And we all know that newlyweds are in the bedroom more often. Older, more mature believers have to calculate their time spent with God. It will happen every morning at 6:45 am. Not to mention every Sunday at 10 am and then, maybe, a spontaneous conference or meeting every now and then. When you're new in your faith, intimacies are not planned; they're just experienced. They happen when they happen. I don't mean to say that we shouldn't have any planned times when we are going to hang with God. But to be intimate should include both the known and the unknown, the usual and the unusual. What makes the bedroom so exciting is the unknown. Detailing the unknown would rob you of the experience of discovery.

One of the big buzzwords these days is the word "experience." I confess I abuse it just as much as the next person. Mainly, it stems from the need to move past the *knowledge* of facts into the journey of them. No longer do I simply want to know. I want to feel what I know, see it, touch it, walk through it, fall in it … experience it. If I asked you if you wanted to experience God, the answer would more than likely be "yes!"

Experiencing God sounds a lot more exciting than just knowing about God (although both sound good). But experiencing Him sounds like there are more of my senses involved. Knowledge of God requires my head, and occasionally my heart. I want the kind of experience that changes the way I look, like Moses coming down from Mount Sinai: his face was shining from being face to face with God—or at least face to His back (God told Moses he couldn't bear to see His face, it would have been too much. So He showed him His back). I want to experience God like that, but somehow I don't think that comes through the usual encounters with Him.

But just as soon as we try and contemplate this image of the bedroom, out pops our mental dictionary to chase it away. If you've come this far in reading, maybe you're not trying to chase out the notion, but perhaps you're looking for a comfortable way to deal with it. You want greater intimacy with God, you want to experience Him, you want to be so relationally close to Him, but your mind keeps getting in the way.

When most people think of the bedroom, they think of sex—and sex is not a word we commonly associate with God. How do we see sex? For some, it looks like a one-night stand; for others, maybe a one-sided fulfillment. It can be an emotionally exhausted refusal, something that's earned or used only as a reward. But remember that even your best experience does not do justice to the Divine. We are speaking of The One who knows us, who created us.

So what happens during sex? What is supposed to happen is one person caring for the other, caring about meeting their needs, desiring to bring them pleasure. And then, theoretically, the same comes in return (or at the same time). In the end, vulnerability happens, openness unlike any other time in our day. If I asked you if you want God to care for you, meet your needs, bring you pleasure and connect with you, you would probably say yes. By letting ourselves be known and getting to know Him, we engage in an intimate encounter. We are used to calling this an "experience" with God. We want to know the way to a deeper relationship with God. But a deeper way is often a different way. And a different way is often unknown and uncomfortable—at least at first.

When I first started to think about this new image of God, I was scared. I'm still a little scared. Maybe you are too. What will people think? What would my mother think? "Oh, yes Mom, I'm writing a book. ... What's that you ask? What is it about? Let's see how can I put this nicely? It's about, ummm, well, it's about ... sex with God." Phone cuts off.

My mother grew up, and still is, Coptic Orthodox. The Coptic Orthodox church is a Christian church, steeped in tradition and the richness of Scripture. There is a reason for everything they do. But my mom grew up in a generation that did not question anything. When I ask her why she thinks something in the church is the way it is, she says, "Because that's the way it has always been." I love the faith my parents have. They believe—and there is little to move that belief. Believe me, I've tried.

But despite the fact that this is not a common topic in churches or the fact that people might blush over it, I can't get it out of my head. Maybe that's because it does seem forbidden. But being different for different's sake isn't appealing to me anymore. I believe this idea will not leave my mind and heart because it opens the door for more—more than what I think, more than I have experienced, more than what people say. I do know that no one can fulfill me like God. There is more. Not more of God, because He is already given us all of Himself. There is more that I can let go of, and thus there is more I can experience of Him.

I want more. There has to be more: More than just a one-time encounter with God. More than a vow before all men that I would honor, love and cherish Him for the rest of my life. More than just a tidy wedding picture, framed by comfort and control.

I felt as though my relationship with God had halted at the front steps of the church. I wasn't allowing myself to go any further. My relationship with God got all dressed up in flannel pajamas and neatly laid in the other twin bed in the room, only to be awoken, strapped into a suit of tradition and sent on its way to do as everyone else does. But for anyone that ever watched *Leave it to Beaver*, you know there comes a time when the nightstand gets moved and the twin beds get pushed together.

I'm sick of looking into churches and seeing the same cookie-cutter mold Christians. We in the church are partly to blame. We take the new and excited believer and put them back in their bridal gown and put God back in His tux and tell them to be intimate, but never let them take their clothes off. I'm sorry, but if verbal intimacy were the only intimacy I had with my husband—we'd need a counselor. It's true we either reveal the whole truth about God, allowing Him to stand naked before us and us awkwardly clothed, or we reveal the whole truth about ourselves and let God remain clothed, and both of us feel awkward. God designed us to be naked and unashamed.

At the end of God creating man and woman, Moses writes that Adam and Eve *were both naked and were not ashamed* (Genesis 2:25). What a feeling that must have been. To not have the formality of clothes between them, hiding who they truly were. How amazing that they could stand there and not be afraid of what the other person thought or saw. It speaks of them being naked in both a physical and spiritual state—because after they sin they tried to hide, physically and spiritually, from God. They sewed fig leaves together to cover their physical nakedness. They wished to cover up their spiritual bodies with a lie. It was the first time God was naked and we were clothed. How sad God must have felt that day.

God made man, and in doing so He realized that even though He had supplied every known need, man still felt lonely. He needed companionship. So God made Eve; she fulfilled this need for companionship, and it didn't interfere with Adam's relationship with God, or hers. There was not a struggle to place one over the other. Scripture takes the time to define the relationship between Adam and Eve. We know they were naked and unashamed. We know they had every need met. We even know that they had their need for physical intimacy met. Genesis uses a specific word to describe this sexual encounter, *yada*, which in its simplest form is not defined as sex, but "to know."

This word also can be defined as "to know by experience." *Experience*. This word is what is used to describe Adam and Eve without their fig leaves on. Is that the type of experience you were asking for? Is that how you want to know and experience God? Or is that too much ... is that too far?

We want to *experience* so many things in our lives. I remember praying to God asking that He wouldn't return until I got married and had sex. I know that's pretty immodest of me to say, but it's true. Then I went on to ask for Him not to come until I had my first child, and then my second child. Now my prayer is that He would come before my daughter goes to junior high; who wants to deal with junior high? (I'm starting a club: all those in favor get "Jesus Before Junior High" bracelets.) But I realized that my prayers were selfish. They revolved around my experiences and the ones I had yet to experience. I wanted options, and I wanted them on my terms. But when will we begin to ask about what God wants, what His desires are? How did God imagine our relationship to work?

There is a give and take between a couple in the bedroom, and as the years pass, it's supposed to get better. Has your relationship with God gotten better? For a married couple, perhaps looks mattered at first, but things grew deeper over time. There were long talks and things spoken in the silence. There was a mutual affection and fulfillment. Awkwardness no longer filled the room, but they begin to experience true intimacy. This is still hard for me to grasp, let alone write about and reveal to people. He longs for us, He chases us, He calls out to us. God is more than just a great friend; He is our Lover. And for years we have denied Him—and ourselves—this pleasure, this intimacy.

A bride and bridegroom weren't meant to stay in their dress and tux forever. Immediately, they were supposed to strip off those formalities and reveal all truth to each other, naked and unashamed. I see God as my Bridegroom. I know that although I have not been the faithful counterpart to Him, He still loves me and I am still His bride. I see this image anew, not stuffy and in still life as I had pictured it before. Now God and I are real, the formal clothes removed, and God is lifting me up and taking me into a place where I have never been before: the bedroom.

One of the most controversial books in God's word is the *Song of Solomon*, and yet it is included in the canon of Scripture. At church we sing of God as the "Lover of our souls," but do we mean it? Do we even know what that means? Song of Solomon is one of the books that confirms this image of God as our Lover. God included it in the Bible so that we would know that "yes, it's okay to see God this way!" He knew that we would question this picture of our relationship. He foresaw the Christian culture that would deny this image.

It is a book of love; it is a book of passion and pleasure. The young woman in the book is talking to her lover and she says, *Take me with you. Come, let's run! Bring me into your bedroom, O my king* (Song of Songs 1:7). Now that's a picture of a married couple that we can relate to. It's anxiousness, an impatience to be closer. Do you feel that? Do you want that? Yes, there are heights and valleys. But have we ever allowed ourselves to grow in that direction? Could this be true for us? Is God allowing us to imagine Him as our Lover? The passion, the pleasure, the union—can that exist in a relationship with God?

If you are still stuck on the idea of God as our Lover, if all you can think about is "this is about sex with God," then you are more than welcome to put on your flannel pajamas and shut this book, never to venture this far from your safe dictionary again. But for those reading on, imagine what this could mean in your relationship with God. Imagine what is missing in your relationship. You can experience a new freedom with God. You don't have to have a relationship with Him that looks like everyone else's.

For so long my relationship has been in the bathroom and not the bedroom. You've heard of those women who never let their husbands see them untidy. They are up before their husbands—fed, showered, and dressed. They would not dare let their spouse see them in an unkempt state. Sounds exaggerated, but we do that with our faith. I have cleaned my faith up, changed its outfit, sprayed on perfume … all ways to make it renewed and refreshed … all attempts to make it go deeper. Don't think this applies to you? Just think about the way you represent your faith when you go to church, or better yet, when you talk to an unbeliever. Our faith was meant for the journey, not for a plated glass box in a museum. And until you are comfortable with that thought, you will never move past the same block you've walked with God.

I've gotten comfortable with God in the living room of my life. I've dined with Him, sharing all that has happened in my day and what was on my mind. I've experienced Him in almost every room of my life—except the bedroom (unless you count sleeping in church). I want more, and I think it is behind the bedroom door.

This is where it starts, with a paradigm shift. The mind is the gateway to the heart. If you have just allowed yourself to imagine the implications of what this could mean in your relationship with God, then you have taken a step closer to opening up those gates and experiencing His flood.

Are you ready to accept Him as your Husband? Because only those married to Him can be intimate with Him. Go ahead; say "I do."

Or renew your vow to Him. You can be assured that His "I do" has already been spoken.

chapter five | **seed**

We are told not to judge a book by its cover, but most of us do. What we see is what we often assume we get, that "it is what it is." These cultural clichés weave seamlessly into our conversations and explanations of circumstances, but we miss the reality of how they have shaped us. They affect how we interact with people, carry out our jobs, hold conversations, interpret what we read and even mold our expectations of others. As Jesus walked this Earth, His goal was not to conform it, but to redefine it. Not to adjust the culture, but define a new one. We read Jesus saying, "You've heard it said …" And then He opens up a new door of possibilities and opportunities with just three words: "But I say …" Redefine. Taking the norm and challenging it. Looking at the common experiences of life and elevating them.

Take the idea of losing one of your sheep. Having sheep was common; maybe even losing one, now and again. Not so common to us, perhaps, but common to the shepherd in the crowd. But then His advice, *go after one of them and leave ninety-nine behind*—not so common (Luke 15:4). Or consider the Last Supper. Jesus took common table elements, bread and wine, to represent the uncommon act of an innocent man's crucifixion (Luke 22:7-20). Sacred elements turned common because the yearly celebration had become ritual. Why did He do this? So that they would see the depth behind the rituals, not just then, but every year they sat and ate—every. It would have been like Jesus giving a deeper meaning to our Thanksgiving stuffing or Christmas ham. The elements were the means to an end for Jesus. Common elements, used for an uncommon purpose.

But what happens when the uncommon affects my comfortable, common world? Take the idea of the seed. Mentioned in all four of the gospels, this idea of a seed really made me think. What if the seed means more than I have always thought it to be? What if changing my common approach to the seed produces an uncommon result in my spiritual journey?

Jesus talks to the people about a farmer who is sowing some seed (Matthew 13:3-23).[4] The seed falls on four different soils and produces four different results. Jesus goes on to explain how the seed is God's word and the soil is the heart: same seed, different responses in different people's hearts. It's a great story, and Jesus explains it so we can understand it. So now every time we see the word "seed" in God's

---

4   Mark 4:3-20; Luke 8:4-15; John 1:1-5,14

Word, we think farmer, or fruit, or plants, or something agricultural. But what if I told you that the Greek word for "seed" is the word *sperma*? Now calm down. I'm not trying to demoralize the Bible. The farmer story is still a story about planting seeds, but it does make one think about the potential meanings of other verses.

> *Those who have been born of God do not sin, because GOD'S SEED abides in them; they cannot sin because they have been born of God.*
>
> -I John 3:9, NRSV

If seed can mean more than I have know, then there is also a seed that says, "I have been intimate with the Father and the proof of it is inside me." And soon it will show. It may be hard to tell at first, but eventually people won't be able to deny the evidence.

I'm going to go out on a limb and guess that you know how babies are made. No one would ask a pregnant woman, "How did this happen?" On the other hand, take a believer in Christ who is carrying something that God has placed within them and watch them go public with it. We'll ask, "So, how did this happen?" Why is spiritual reproduction such a vague concept? Why are we not used to people being impregnated with something from God?

> *In the same way my friends, you have died to the law through the body of Christ, so that*

who has been raised from the dead in order
that WE MAY BEAR FRUIT FOR GOD.
-Romans 7:4, NRSV, emphasis mine

I like to belong. I like the fact that when I came to accept Christ as my Savior, there was so much more I came into: I gained a Savior, a Lord, a Father, a Friend, a Husband and a Lover. I *want* to belong to God. I want to reproduce spiritually what He has sown in me. That's what it means to bear fruit for God. But God is a gentleman. He does not force Himself upon us. Augustine, famous bishop of Hippo, wrote, "Without God we cannot, without us he will not."[5] Augustine speaks of a divine politeness: when we are ready, He is waiting for us.

My mother had three miscarriages. One of those miscarriages was in her fifth month of pregnancy. She thinks she miscarried because she put a warm bottle of water on her stomach when she was aching. I told her she was wrong, that it was not her fault. Miscarriages mean that the environment was not right to grow a baby.

You've been there—the retreat, the Sunday morning service. Commitments made; a month later, a commitment forgotten. Sometimes we ask God to plant a seed in us that we are not ready for. But we insist. And the seed fails to implant, fails to "link" to us. We weren't ready. Miles Stanford in his book *The Green*

5   Foster, Richard. *Streams of Living Water*. New York: HarperSanFrancisco, 2001. 197. Print.

When sin entered the picture, it was like God finding out we were in fertile.

Letters wrote, "For some years now the evangelistic scene has been dominated by a conversion known as 'commitment,' which often, sad to say, amounts to little more than a spiritual miscarriage."[6]

Maybe we did it for people and not God, or maybe we thought we were ready for God's seed, but He wasn't (that's why it takes two to make a baby). Sin could exist in our lives. And where there is sin, God is not there; even His seed will not remain. For whatever reason, the environment (that would be you and me) was not suitable for growth.

So what environment is? *But now abide faith, hope, love, these three; but the greatest of these is love* (1 Corinthians 13:13). And The One who is love sent His Son in love. Now when we accept that gift, His blood covers our wombs. That cleansing that happens to a woman monthly is what prepares her womb for the seed. Jesus' blood cleanses us, and enables us to carry the seed God gives us.

I had an abortion. Four little words that don't seem to grasp all that my choice created. The circumstances were hard, and yet fairly typical. I was in my second year of college in Indiana. The first real relationship I had back home—Kenneth—was shelved in hopes of discovering what "true love" really looked like. What I didn't realize was that in physical intimacy, you typically pick up where you left off; in other words,

6   Stanford, Miles J. *The Green Letters*. Grand Rapids, MI: Zondervan, 1975. 39. Print.

you'll go as far (or farther) with a new guy as you did with the last one.

College was a new arena for me. Back home I was used to being "just Irini." I hung out with guys all the time, but boyfriends were few and far between. But when I went to college, guys noticed me. It was all new to me, and I liked it. I soon came to realize that all guys are not the same. In one particular relationship where verbal and emotional intimacy lacked, I tried to make up for it physically. I kept trying to make the "too far" line more and more vague. I mean, who could really say when you crossed it? I knew. My heart knew.

This is the part of the story where I wish I could say I didn't know God yet. I would love if this were my testimony *before* I met Jesus—but it isn't. I had an abortion while I was saved, at a Christian college, dating a Christian man, called into ministry and studying for a double major in Christian Ministries and Business. I got pregnant the first time I had sex.

I wanted to do the right thing and keep the baby, just to please everyone. But I really didn't want to. I couldn't match this present reality with what I thought was my future destiny, so I changed the one I thought I was in control of. It was my choice. I can't blame anyone else for it; I wanted to do it. There are no more ways to tiptoe around it so that it doesn't sound as hard and selfish as it really was.

It's hard to admit our failures, my failures. But out of it I believe God has shown—and is still showing—His redemption. The enemy would love for me to keep quiet about this part of my life. When you look at my Christmas card, my family looks perfect. I am very blessed to be married to such a wonderful man and to have such amazing children. It would be easier to leave this story in my past, to make up some nice thing about past failures and how God has forgiven me and set me free. But I want you to know about my Husband, God, who chooses to forget my past and embrace me. Despite my failures, He is still for me. Remember that battle for intimacy? *We will overcome by the blood of the Lamb and the word of our testimony* (Revelation 12:11). The *blood of the Lamb* was shed when Jesus died on the cross. All that is needed to overcome is the words of our testimonies to be spoken, to release victory in our battles. When I speak what my Husband has done for me, of His extravagant love, it sets slaves free to become brides. God is redeeming my false intimacies for the truest intimacy, and He longs to do the same for you.

Part of my redemption to this story has been an image of how we can have spiritual abortions. I don't use this imagery lightly, and I hope you see that I understand it deeply. There are times when we welcome God's seed; but when things seem wrong or uncomfortable or inconvenient, we abort it. Spiritual abortion often occurs at the feet of pride. It's like we welcome what He wants to plant within us, but on our own terms. We ask God if He could put it in someone else and then we could just manage them, help them take care of it. Then we wouldn't be so inconvenienced by the pregnancy, the labor and then the ultimate delivery of the promise—the birth. But if God has a seed intended for you to carry, He does not believe in a surrogate.

Many years after my abortion, I had a baby. During a visit to the emergency room early in the pregnancy, they said I had miscarried. But they were wrong. God enabled my daughter to fight to stay attached to me, and she was born on June 12, 2003.

God gave me this picture of spiritual pregnancy while I was physically pregnant with my daughter. He told me how He had planted a seed in me, just like when my daughter was conceived. And I received that seed, I accepted that seed, I allowed that seed to grow and become one with me. God has been taking His time with the spiritual pregnancy I'm in the midst of right now. I feel like I have been spiritually pregnant with something that He planted in me a long time ago. I just want to finally see the fruit—get this baby out! I want to hold it and smile and say, "Thank you God. This was worth it all."

But I have to realize that as soon as God breaks my water and allows the seed He planted in me and the fruit of my labor to be seen, I will have to wake up in the middle of the night to its cry. The next day, I will have to feed it and help it develop. One day it will get sick. One day it will be mad at me. One day it will tell me it loves me. But that's just it: it will never go away. It is something that God placed in me to give birth to and now I am responsible for it—every day.

and now I am responsible for it—every day.

The reason why there is such a shock for new parents is that the baby doesn't have an "off" button. You prepared for the baby: you made a room, picked out clothes for him, people celebrated with you and now he's in your arms. But all of a sudden, four arms (or sometimes, just two) don't seem like enough. You need reinforcements. It's harder than it seems. It feels like you're going crazy. You wanted to give birth to this promise, this seed that God placed in you, but this is hard! (I don't sound like I've been there before, do I?)

God doesn't want us to give birth to something that we are not willing to take care of. As if I have not already crossed every blasphemous line possible in my spiritual descriptions, I have one more daring thought. Not only do we sometimes not create the right environment and miscarry God's seed or refuse His seed and abort it, sometimes we use protection with God. When do people use protection? When they don't want to get pregnant. How many of us just want the intimacy with God without the responsibility that goes with it? We want spiritual protection, a guarantee (like 96%) that we can have intimacy with God on our terms. And for the most part, we all know that anything on *our terms* never turns out right. But we were born in sin and it is that sin mentality in which we must battle with everyday. We are a new creation, but we have to retrain our soul (mind, will and emotions) and our body to submit to our re-born spirit. Our sin nature wants us to get what is good for ourselves. We have goes against our "survival of the fittest" mentality.

How have we protected ourselves? For some it could be in how we have viewed God, thinking of Him as only Judge or Defender and not as a Lover. Others protect themselves by only believing what they want to in the scriptures, creating a gospel of convenience. Many times we think we are protecting ourselves by not listening or obeying what we know God has asked us to do. Protection is really our way of prevention. What do we want to prevent? The unknown.

In an imperfect world, beautiful babies are born to imperfect parents every day. The same occurs in the spiritual world: God lets us give birth, even though we have no idea what we are doing. But that's just it: God did not ask you to give birth and then be a single parent. He helped in its creation, and He wants to help in its development. It's *His* seed. He does not want you just for the seed you can carry for Him; He wants *you*. He wants to be close to you. The seed is just a result of your intimacy.

We don't live in a world where family is celebrated; instead, we live in a world where everything fights against the family unit. Between work, school, sport practice, music lessons, church, charity and a social life, who has time to sit down at the dinner table and talk? As I am writing this, the New Year has arrived and new goals are emerging for our family. But to be honest, most of them are very independent and selfish goals. I say all of that to say that it is hard to co-create with God. We aren't wired to share, to ask for help, to look out for others. I can't think of a more hostile environment for God's seed than in my flesh.

When I was pregnant, I remember being worried about everything—especially physically. What if I fell? What if I ate too much folic acid? What if I ate too little? What if I got in an accident? But my doctor reassured me, telling me that it is hard to hurt the seed inside of me. She was so well protected by my body and the sac surrounding her that I could rest assured in her safety. Our flesh is the worst place for the growth of God's seed, but God gave us His Son, so that His righteousness could surround God's seed and give it hope for survival. My old self would not have been the place for God's seed to thrive, but thank God that I am a new creation.

God invests deeply into spiritual reproduction. To begin with, He reproduced Himself in us. *And God created man in His own image, in the image of God He created him; male and female He created them* (Genesis 1:27). That is one reason why we should deal carefully with one another; we each carry a piece of His image. Only collectively can we see the fullness of God.

Then, how about the way God used to bring forth His Son? Why hassle with going through the natural means to bring forth the Messiah? Let's be real here: Jesus could have just appeared somehow. He could have been in a basket on Mary's doorstep. But instead, God took the common means of reproduction and inserted His uncommon approach. He took Mary's willingness and His will, and brought forth Jesus.

This is the ultimate picture of God planting His seed in us. Mary could have said no. But I think God would have been just as comfortable using Susan, Sarah, Nicole, or Amy—someone who said "Yes." God wants to reproduce in us, but if we refuse His seed, His plan and purposes will move on. And while He would love for us to be a part of it all, He respects your choice; that's why He gave it to you. Your affections are the only thing that He can't control—and are the very thing heaven and earth are in a battle over.

God thinks in reproductive terms. That doesn't sound exciting; it actually sounds like a bad biology class. But what it means is that He is always thinking about reaching more people, touching more lives, having more people know Him. So when He lost us in the garden, He created a way to get us back—through Jesus. And the way Jesus explained things, we all need a re-birth, a second chance at this thing called life. To Nicodemus this idea seemed absurd. How on earth could he enter back into his mother's womb and be reborn? (I agree with Nicodemus here: I am not re-entering my mother's womb.) But Jesus gives another twist to common wisdom. You say you're only born once, I say you can be born again—*by water and the Spirit* (John 3:5). The *water* refers to water baptism, and *the Spirit* is referring to baptism by the Holy Spirit, the third person in the Trinity.

God wanted to reach more of us. He wanted more of us to know Him and enter into a relationship with of us to know Him and enter into a relationship with Him. When sin entered the picture, it was like God finding out we were infertile. No matter how much God and I want to reproduce something together, if there is unrepentant sin in my life, I am infertile. When Hosea was angry at Israel for betraying God, He asked God to punish them. *Give them, O Lord—what will you give them? Give them wombs that miscarry and breasts that are dry* (9:14). What could be worse than having intimacy with God that reproduces nothing in our lives? Or what about a responsibility that we are incapable of nourishing and feeding so that it can grow?

Hosea was speaking of Israel in a physical sense. He wanted Israel to die off because they were a disgrace to God. When we only think about ourselves and not about how we can reproduce what God has planted in us, we are missing it. We are missing the way God thinks, the way He loves, the reason He shared His seed with us. What would Satan's greatest wish for us be? That we would be selfish and infertile all our lives. The Hebrew word for miscarry, *nephel*, can be translated as *fallen*. We have all heard of someone having "fallen" away from God. But how does that happen, where does it start? Maybe by being infertile.

So how do we get from being infertile to fertile? By being re-born. Jesus told Nicodemus to be reborn by water and by Spirit (John 3:5). The water was through baptism. In baptism, we have the recognition declaration of our dedication to Him. Baptism is an image of our spiritual marriage to God. He's there, you're there, and people are there to witness it. Maybe we should start throwing birdseed at the end of a baptismal service.

We were born hostile to God. But God says, "Let me birth you anew through the Holy Spirit." *That which is born of the flesh is flesh, and that which is born of the Spirit is spirit* (John 3:6). I have already been born of the flesh; I want something else. If I am going to be reborn, I want to be a product of the Spirit. This is the second baptism, when we are immersed in the Holy Spirit. The Holy Spirit is the seal to our new birth and the sort of *Jiminy Cricket* to our journey. Dying to ourselves, marriage to God, and the seal of the Holy Spirit—we need them for rebirth AND we need them for spiritual reproduction.

Why all this trouble to make us renewed or to send His Son? I don't know. That's profound to say, I'm sure. All I know is that this image of His seed and the beauty of reproduction keep coming up over and over again in His Word. (When my mother wanted to get her point across, she would repeat herself—in both languages.) I think in these repetitions we are discovering a point God is trying to get across to us as the Church—as His bride. He is speaking it through His Word and through your spirit.

Am I willing to carry His seed? That's the question I ask myself. Am I willing to engage with God in such a powerful and passionate manner that I will sacrifice my conveniences, my selfishness, my schedule, my time, my goals, my dreams … myself? Am I willing to die in order for His Seed to be placed inside of me?

Dying to self: do I have to go there? I speak of "death to self" because that is what happened to me when I became a parent. I remember asking a good friend of mine when things got back to normal for her after she had her baby boy (keep in mind I had just had my little girl; I needed some reassurance). She paused, and then very gently told me that life would never be the same. I would never be the same. I remember how disheartening that sounded, like finding out I'd lost someone very near to me. But now, looking back almost nine years later, I'm glad I will never be the same. Sure, Satan tempts me by trying to make me think I had it "good" then; but I know the truth. I know the joy that my little girl, and now my son, have become.

I also know who I've become in the process of carrying, laboring, delivering and caring for those seeds. I'm better. To be honest, that is why many of you are reading this: to get better. But God's desire for you is not to get better; it's to get closer … to Him. But God has an uncommon way of helping us get there.

Some of us only want God for the highs He can deliver. Our relationship with Him moves from one mountaintop experience to another. And because we are not willing to give up our selves to carry His seed, another intimate moment God has shared with His creation will die. We are either creating an with His creation will die. We are either creating an environment where the seed can grow, or we are not—and it will die. I'm not saying we get only one chance, but we do only have one short lifetime to work with. God is not interested in a one-night stand with us. He has eternity in mind. He has a seed that He wants to place within us that will help us to see our gifts, talents, personalities and passions bloom.

Stanford in *The Green Letters* writes, "A seed embodies in full the reproduction of the life from which it came."[7] What God wants to place in you has both the DNA of you and God. It is one thing to know the gifts God has given you; it is an entirely different arena to parent that gift in something else besides yourself. I know myself pretty well. I know how I tick. I know what I like and what I do not like. I get me. Now, I have a seed that has come to fruition. And that seed carries my DNA. Those seeds are my daughter and my son. And while they may look like my husband, they have a whole lot of me on the inside. But having to parent your DNA in someone else really grows your understanding of who you are—and how God sees you. You will never truly understand why you are the way you are until you carry and care for the seed He has designed just for you.

For me, carrying the seed has been exciting, but that is where I remain for right now. I am so anxious for the birth of this seed. I feel like I have been pregnant with it for 18 years. Preparations have

---

7   Standford, Miles J. Ibid. 25. Print.

taken their sweet time. People have crossed my path to encourage and develop me for the journey ahead. Mountaintops and valleys have been sprinkled along my path. And I truly don't know which part of all this waiting is my laboring, and which is just a rocky part of the pregnancy. But what I do know is that in His time, it will be born and His promise for me will be actualized. Then I will have the daily responsibility to care for it and nurture it, cry for it and develop it. I will have to be patient and flexible. Some days will fly by and some will creep, and God will be right there helping me take care of what He specifically designed for me to carry, deliver and care for.

It will be beautiful, and it will be hard. I will long for the days when I could just dream about this thing and not have to work it out. I will seek intimacy with God like I used to, but will find He wants to show me something different. But that is what carrying His seed enables me to do—to go further with Him.

chapter six | truth

Who you *really* are will eventually come out, and there is no other relationship like marriage to move that process along. In a friendship, you can put forth whatever image you would like. Even close friends aren't around you every day, all the time. Your family has seen some of your ugly side, but still can be limited to how much they know you. And work relationships; do I really need to explain how they don't always know the real you?

But marriage is another playing field. Marriage has all of the elements of friendship, family, co-workers and more; it's designed to bring out the real you.

I come from a long line of healthy eaters, and I don't mean organic, flaxseed, gluten-free, etc. I mean that we love to eat. Eating is connected to everything: our faith, our culture, our emotions, our celebrations ... you name it and there is a food for it. This was fine for me since I got some height from my mom's side of the family and ran track in high school.

High school is when I met Kenneth; we ran track together. For the next six years we dated off and on (which means I would become unsure, break up with Kenneth and he would hold the box of tissues while I cried). Needless to say, when we got married at 22 we knew a lot about each other. But what Kenneth didn't know was my love and connection to food. Unhealthy connections to food are hard to see when there is no physical evidence.

Now Kenneth loves to enjoy food as well, but he has the gift of self-control. He does not eat in order to make a happy plate—or even a happy mother-in-law (believe me, she's tried). He eats until he is content, not full. He works out and loves it. He does enjoy Blue Bell Homemade Vanilla ice cream like every good Texan should (with cookies, of course). But he never goes too far. He doesn't eat out of an emotional void. He rarely looks at food as more than food. But I go too far. I eat out of an emotional void. I look at food as more than food.

In a good marriage, your spouse can strengthen your weaknesses. Even though you don't like it, they stay the course. Even when you get mad at them for bringing it up, they point you to your goal. Even when you want them to stop, they ask you if that is really what you want them to do. So while I would love that second helping, to eat out of boredom or whatever current emotion is present, or let food become a necessity for gatherings, I am rethinking my choices.

Why? Because I don't want to be the same person I was last year, last month or even last week, and I'm letting Kenneth help me.

That is what God intended when He asked us to marry Him. In a good marriage, the real you is able to come out—for better or for worse, in sickness and in health. But marriage also doesn't let you stay the same; it betters you. This chapter is about you. It is about how you perceive yourself. It is about the truth of how God sees you. No one can improve what they don't know or can't see. Who is the real you? How are you seeing yourself? And what does being married to God have to do with it?

Self. It's who we love the most and yet at times feel like we want to run away from. Our self is so consuming. It begs for attention. So we give in to it—often. But we don't want to be the only ones thinking about ourselves, so we invite people into our lives to give our self some more attention. And whether we do it consciously or not, we want others to see us, to take notice. But what they see—their perception—we hope will be that of what we are striving to be and not necessarily what we are right now. We care what other people think about us, although we know only God's opinion matters.

Colleges and workplaces have you take personality tests to gain a general understanding of who you are. But the reality is that most people answer the questions on the test based on the person they want to become or hope to be perceived as, not as they truly are. Because the truth of who we are may not be acceptable to others—or to ourselves. Although we claim to know ourselves best, it is still our selves that we can't be honest with. There is a lot within us that we don't like.

It's not so easy to recognize this flaw in us. It's actually easier to write it on this page. On this page, it's in black and white. I can get around it. In my own life, I find ways to hide the realities I don't want to see. Take the reality of sin for example. Some sins I recognize, ask for forgiveness and move on. "I said something mean to you, and I am sorry." Other sins I don't think I struggle with, so I dismiss them. If they creep up, I justify them by claiming them as shortcomings or bad days: "My daughter is driving me crazy. She makes me so angry that I have to yell at her just to get her attention." So who am I? Who are you? Are we only what people see? Are we only what we see?

Our society has taught us to believe that "perception is reality." But perceived truth is not the same as real truth. Let my driving prove this point to you. One evening, I set out to pick my sister up from the airport. Having lived in the large city of Dallas, Texas for only a few months, I realized it was a dangerous task to do alone; not because of crime or fear of the unknown, but because Dallas roads are notorious for bringing confusion, and the road signs don't help. As my sister got into the car, I smiled and declared, "It will be a miracle if we get home." We laughed and set out on our journey.

You cannot find the real you when you don't know what is real within you.

The trip should have taken about 25 minutes, max. We left the airport on the route that I *perceived* as the right direction. I even had a map. Although my sister and I both had doubts, I drove on. She pointed to a motor speedway that she could have sworn was in Fort Worth, but I told her she was wrong. My evidence: a sign for Highway 35 South. "I told you we were going the right way. I know this highway, it takes us straight to my house."

And so we continued in our *perceived* truth. To convince my self further, I pointed to a city skyline and attributed it to being downtown Dallas. Now over an hour from when we began, I still felt as though I was going the right way. But I wasn't. No matter how much I *perceived* we were going in the right direction, the real truth was that we were not. We were in Fort Worth, that *was* the motor speedway and the skyline was not Dallas'. As much as I rationalized away why it was the Dallas highway and signage's fault, the reality was that I was not where I thought I was; I was lost. But I kept making decisions based upon my *perception* that I thought was reality.

Reality is what it is; it can't be changed. However, if it becomes distorted or perceived in any other manner, then it is no longer reality. Eventually, hopefully, it will intersect with the real truth. Discovering who you really are involves a sorting process. We have to begin to sort out what is truth and what is everything else (perceptions, lies, misunderstood circumstances and so on). You cannot find the real you when you don't know what is real within you.

"What you see is what you get." We know that is not true. But day after day we make decisions about our lives, about our selves, about each other, based on what we "see." When we haven't sorted through to find out what is real and what isn't, it's like we are standing in front of a mirror in a fun house. There's the funny one, the fat one, and of course, the thin one that we all really like standing in front of. Our choice is based on which perspective we like, and accept it as the true reality.

But imagine that you took the skinny one home. Imagine that was the one you looked into everyday, the one you began to believe was the truth. It would change you: what you wear, what you eat, even how you think. But as much as you hope for it to be the truth, it is not.

It is well known that honesty is one of the keys to a great relationship, but we avoid that mirror. It doesn't feel good. It makes me uncomfortable. I feel inconvenienced. But you cannot change what you cannot see. So as you have tried to draw closer with God and have failed, then a look in the mirror is what you need. Not that fun house mirror you took home; an honest mirror. Maybe it's a friend's mirror or a co-worker's, maybe a pastor's or even a spouse's mirror. The only thing that matters is that it is a mirror that reveals God's truth: it convicts you, but it never condemns you. God wants to show you things in order to better you. He does not desire to bring you down

and make you feel guilty. Guilt gets you nowhere, but conviction pushes you forward.

Take a good look in that mirror. See the truth. The truth is that God is crazy about you. He made the earth and everything in it—for you. He saw Creation as "good" and, once you were in the picture, as "very good." The truth is that God pursues you everyday. He is there when you wake up. He walks beside you, stands next to you, sits close to you, lays with you. The truth is that you were worth giving up something He absolutely loved in order for you to be truly intimate. Because that is what love does, it sacrifices for the other. Even though our separation was our own fault, He made a way to bring us back together. The truth is that He doesn't get caught up in your faults the way you do. He sees them, yes, but only as roadblocks to getting closer to you. He wants them gone so He can be intimate with you again; you, not the person you are going to be or all the things you want to do for Him. He wants to be close to who you are right now.

God reveals things in our lives so that we draw closer to becoming all He destined us to be. So stop trying to be somebody you are not. Stop trying to compare yourself to the next person in the pew or the gym, at work or in the bank. We measure our lives to Jesus', not another friend or a church member. Our comparisons contribute to our false perception of how close we are with Him. We measure intimacy by how much closer we are to Jesus than others *appear* to be.

Another faulty perception is when we look at things in the rearview mirror, as if we measure our relationship with God by the last close encounter we had with Him. So if last year you had an amazing altar call encounter with Him, then that is where your intimacy level is; as if you could pick up where you left off. Others look at their past and determine that they or God will not allow for intimacy to occur because of their failures, but *these are distorted mirrors.* Do you see how Satan would love for you to live in this false reality? The longer he can keep you from seeing the real you, the farther he keeps you from your Lover. God longs to be real with us, but we must believe there is another mirror, a true one.

At some point, whether during courting or within the first year of marriage, couples try to decipher how real they are allowed to be with their partner. Women eating only salads on their dates are stuck trying to introduce their real appetites to their husbands. Men who were taught to always act like everything is under control have to determine if they can tell their wives about a financial struggle. But as the days turn to weeks turn to months turn to years, most façades fade away. Each day, couples are faced with an opportunity to be open and honest ... to be real. And so it is with God. We must take the time not only to read God's Word and to pour our hearts out to Him, but to linger there. It is in that lingering that the Holy Spirit is free to take what we've read and heard, revealing a supernatural perspective on our lives.

While reading the book of Amos, I was trying to really understand what was going on. I had been reading other Old Testament books and was having a hard time getting over the redundancy of the sin cycle. I kept reading over and over about how God called out to His people, and they ignored Him. God warned them, they returned, they messed up again. But it wasn't until I got to Amos that I was open to the Holy Spirit showing me God's true hatred for sin. This seems like a basic foundational truth. Give me a multiple-choice test and I would be able to pick out what God does not like the most: bunnies, chocolate or sin. But as I lingered there, the Holy Spirit revealed to me that I have a selective hatred of sin. I hate the sin of child abuse. I hate the sin of adultery. I hate the sin of hypocrisy. Those were easy sins to hate—because they were sins that I did not struggle with.

But the sin of pride—yes, I hated it, but only when I was honest enough to recognize it. The rest of the time I had it camouflaged as confidence or security. But the Holy Spirit revealed to me that I was to hate that sin as much as I hated the sin of rape, that it was just as damaging.

I chose to let God reveal His truth to me. And because of that face-to-face encounter, His truth has now become my truth. His true reality is now mine as well, and I am better for it. That's what intimacy does: it betters us. Too often we fear the truth because we innately believe that it might destroy the person—the self—we've grown attached to. We may not like who we are, but for many, we would choose to sticking with the self we know, faults and all, rather than risk relinquishing our self to end up with the unknown. We think, *What if God does all of this revealing and in the end, I don't like the real me?* But who created us? Who knit every detail into our lives? Who was the one who gave us our desires? Surely He is able to restore us to His original creation. He must know how to grow and change us without disregarding our desires.

Satan has fooled us into believing that all truth is painful. But God's Word reminds us that with truth comes freedom from the lies that have shackled our understanding, from our vision of our selves (John 8:32). We have made so many decisions based upon those distorted mirrors, and thus we have made choices about what we like and don't like based upon an illusion.

Allowing God to reveal who you really are is a journey into the unknown. Intimacy is gained as you are able to stand in front of the mirror, allowing God to show you things you have ignored. Maybe you need to hear God telling you of each purposeful creation on your physical body; that He intended for you to be that height, with that hair color and those eyes. Maybe you need to hear Him say that yes, you do belong in that family.

The longer you stand there, the deeper you allow Him to go. The things you have purposefully ignored are now seen for what they are. But it is also now that you are equipped with truth about your likes and dislikes, because now you know the real you. How long has it been since you have seen the real you? How many years or decades do you have to go back to find that person? Has the real you ever been allowed to exist? It is when you face truth that things begin to change, because now you're getting to see the real you. And what is so exciting is that the longer you allow this encounter to occur, the closer you are to liking what you see.

Now He can point out that sin you have been justifying.

One day, I tried something strange. It was a Saturday morning; my husband and daughter were gone to the gym and my son was miraculously sleeping in. What would I do with this unanticipated alone time? I decided to read my Bible. That sounds a lot more spiritual than it really was. Mainly I was reading so that if I turned on the television afterwards I wouldn't feel guilty. Having not found a new devotional to plug through, climbing another rung on my spiritual ladder, I had just been meandering through scriptures on marriage. Again, it sounds spiritual, but it was because my husband and I were leading a couples' small group.

I landed in Song of Solomon. Oh yes, the naughty book; the place that every teen eventually discovers, smirking the whole way through. The book in itself is an anomaly in the Bible—or is it? Why was it included in the Bible? *Intimacy.*

Originally called The Song of Songs, it's the

notion that this is the *best of the best songs*. While thinking rationally, this might sound a bit overstated; but when you're in love, it's exactly the right phrase. Think back to when you were young and in love. Or just think back to a great movie about it. This book would be like a couple saying, "They're playing OUR song." You know, the one that a couple believes was written just for them—or at least they acted that way. It was mushy, it was long, and it was perfect; at least until you broke up and then it was too mushy, too long—and far from perfect.

As I sat there, all I could think about were the young man's words to his girl. His descriptions were all the things that he could think of that equaled to beauty and grandeur. But after he speaks them to her, he must have begun to see her in his everyday life. He passes the tower of David and thinks of her neck. He sees doves and thinks of her eyes. A flock of goats reminds him of her hair (Song of Songs 4:1-7, NIV). She doesn't just see her lover in the things around her but she even thinks about how they compare with him: his *love is better than wine* (Song of Solomon, 1:2b). Her lover's love had surpassed what the world had to offer in comfort, in celebration, in riches, in anything. Does your relationship with God affect you like that?

As I sat thinking about God that Saturday morning, I thought about what His love was like to me:

Your love is like a holiday …
Your love is like a Saturday afternoon …

Your love is like chocolate …
Your love is like sleeping in …
Your love is like losing weight and not trying …
Your love is better than people's attention …
Your love is better than getting my list done ...
Your love is better than any position or title …
Your love is better than approval …
Your love is better than my love,
         and yet you still love me.

What is God's love like to you? What do you compare it to? Have you allowed His love to be better than something?

Part of what marriage does is to change our thoughts. Dr. Gary Smalley, well known for his relationship advice, talks about how our thoughts are the starting point for all we believe. Then, from that belief, we act: our emotions, words and actions.[8] When you add up our actions each day, you end up with our habits. So if we want to change our relationship with God, we have to change our thoughts about Him, because our thoughts about Him have been so limiting. He is my Savior, He is my Lord, He is my Friend, He is my Judge. But He also is my Husband and my Lover. Change your thoughts about Him so He can help you change your thoughts about yourself. He doesn't want to get closer to you just to say that He is. He wants to get closer to you because He loves you. And true love

---

8   Smalley, Gary, Dr. *The DNA of Relationships.* Illinois: Tyndale House, 2007. Print.

Krini Jambro

doesn't let us stay the way we are; it helps us get to where we want to be … it betters us.

chapter seven | **cheating**

Why are so many of us caught flirting with someone else? Did you know you could cheat on God? I know you can, because I have. In our minds, there is flirting and then there's cheating—we have made them two separate things. Some unfortunate advice married people often get is that "flirting doesn't hurt" or "you can look, but you can't touch." Cheating on God starts with a look, moves to flirting, then leads you to gathering your clothes around the room.

We don't like this imagery. It's as uncomfortable as imagining ourselves with God in the bedroom. We don't dwell on it long; it makes us squirm. There is no comfortable picture that describes unfaithfulness. He doesn't liken it to a player not being loyal to a team or a worker not persevering in his job. He says, *You adulteress wife, who takes strangers instead of her husband!* (Ezekiel 16:32). If memory serves me correctly, to be adulterous requires involving someone else in the picture.

Enter Satan.

Now we don't call it out like that. We cheat on God with our jobs, our hobbies, our goals or maybe it's our desires. We don't say it like it really is—we are having sex with Satan. Here we are again: squirmy, uncomfortable. But you have to ask yourself, is it true? When we engage in things that draw us away from God, do we often begin to feel closer, more connected to that thing? Does it begin to influence our mind, our will and our emotions?

Think about some of the major purposes of the bedroom: connection and reproduction. Anything can be a tool that Satan uses to seduce you into the bedroom. He can use your drive for a position, he can use your looks, he can use your motherhood, he can use *anything*; that activity you've been connecting to carries the danger of reproduction.

In this world, you are either making connections with God or Satan, and there is no middle ground. When you say "I do" to God, you are saying "I don't" to everything else, but if the position you're going after at work is becoming what defines you, you are knocking at a stranger's door. If it starts to become what you believe will provide for you, you have walked into the enemy's bedroom. If that position becomes all you think about and put effort towards, you are naked and vulnerable and making connecting with a stranger. *You adulteress wife, who takes strangers instead of her husband!* It wasn't the pursuit of the position that was wrong; it was what it did to your relationship with God.

He isn't waiting for you to "get better" before He loves you; He loves you already.

'Everything is permissible for me'—but not everything is beneficial. 'Everything is permissible for me'—but I will not be mastered by anything (I Corinthians 6:12). Paul says yes, you are a grownup, you can do anything you want; that is the nature of God giving us free will. But while everything is permissible, is it beneficial? You cannot make a choice and have it only affect you. Look around. Every relationship you have will be affected by your choices, especially the relationship between you and God. Let's finish the rest of the passage that Paul wrote in I Corinthians 6:12-20:

> 'Everything is permissible for me'—but not everything is beneficial. 'Everything is permissible for me'—but I will not be mastered by anything. 'Food for the stomach and the stomach for food'—but God will destroy them both. The body is not meant for sexual immorality, but for the Lord, and the Lord for the body. By his power God raised the Lord from the dead, and he will raise us also. Do you not know that your bodies are members of Christ himself? Shall I then take the members of Christ and unite them with a prostitute? Never! Do you not know that he who unites himself with a prostitute is one with her in body? For it is said, 'The two will become one flesh.' **But he who unites himself with the Lord is one with**

him in spirit. *Flee from sexual immorality. All other sins a man commits are outside his body, but he who sins sexually sins against his own body. Do you not know that your body is a temple of the Holy Spirit, who is in you, whom you have received from God? You are not your own; you were bought at a price. Therefore honor God with your body.*
(emphasis mine)

Do you see how your relationship with God is not just as Friend, not just as Savior, not just as Lord, but as your Husband, your Lover? That phrase *the two will become one flesh* is a quote from the passage in Genesis 2:24, the marriage of Adam and Eve. Do you need any more evidence that God sees you as His spouse? We see things that are wrong in our lives, and we might even call it sin; but until we see ourselves as married to God, we will never see it as He does: adultery. Everything that comes at you in life is an opportunity to either grow closer to God or farther from Him. It's either His bed, or another's.

Most often adultery doesn't just happen. It's a process, and it starts with a thought: *I wish I had ... I wish she were more ... I want ...* Each thought builds until it grows into a belief that we have: *I'm never going to get this. She is never going to be what I want her to be. I want what I can't have.* All those beliefs that started out with one simple thought are now determining the way we talk, act and feel.

I didn't just wake up one morning and decide that I wanted to let my job in ministry become my identity. It was what I did with each word of encouragement, each success I had and especially the weight I put on people's words over God's. These were all innocent opportunities, but it is what I did with them that left me feeling used and empty. I held on to those encouragements, successes and words a little too closely, letting myself get too connected to them. I had to break the connection, the adulterous place I had let it become. If I did not break the ties, the pride that had begun to grow would soon reproduce in my life.

In the book of Revelation, John conveys a letter from God to each of the seven churches in the province of Asia. The first letter is written to the church in Ephesus. They are the church that was warned of having *left their first love* (Revelation 2:4). Life continued, but their intimacy had ceased. They said 'not tonight' over and over again to God. Instead of talking with God about what we want, what we are struggling with, what we need, like the church at Ephesus—we just roll over. We don't talk about it, but it's on our mind. And what stays on our mind eventually takes residence in our heart. From our hearts come our feelings, words and actions.

Seduction takes time. Just because you aren't thinking about cheating on God doesn't mean someone else isn't. And while in theory we believe Satan is real, we don't act like it. We imagine him like the cartoon sketch of a man in a red costume, pitchfork, tail and all. He is the one on the left shoulder that gives us bad advice. Can I tell you today that he is not trying to be just your friend? He is the guy that parents fear their little girl will meet. He wants to make out with us, use us and then drop us. God gave us free will, but He allows us to choose, and this is what happens when we make the wrong choice, when we run into the arms of another:

> *I will also give you into the hands of your lovers, and they will tear down your shrines, demolish your high places, strip you of your clothing, take away your jewels, and will leave you naked and bare.*
>
> -Ezekiel 16:39

God cannot make you stay in His arms. He gave you the right to choose, even if that means choosing the arms of another; and he only comes back when he wants something from us. He does not care how he gets us, he just wants us. He does not want us because he loves us; he wants us because he hates God. He is the epitome of the one-night stand: selfish, not giving. He is not interested in building relationship. Satan wants to win this spiritual battle against God and he's using you to get there.

This might be a little too direct for you. We have always known that Satan was bad, but not so methodical, intentional or so personal. No one ever talks about the relationship he wants to have with you. He knows that we're relational creatures by nature;

relationship is where he can have the greatest impact.

After you say "I do" to God, Satan starts planning; his plans for seduction are detailed and personalized. Satan can't read your mind, but most often he doesn't need to. Remember, your feelings, words and actions are a reflection of your heart, what's really inside of you. So he watches what you do, what you say, what you buy, what you spend your time on. To entice someone, to seduce them, he makes himself very familiar with what they think they want.

What would Satan use to entice you? Take a look at what consumes your thoughts, your feelings, your time, your words. These things can all start off at safe, godly places, but where could they go if taken to the extreme? He can—and will—even use the things God gives us. Read how God tells Ezekiel to explain to His people about their relationship:

> Then I passed by you and saw you, and behold, you were at the time for love; so I spread My skirt over you and covered your nakedness. I also swore to you and entered into a covenant with you so that you became Mine, declares the Lord GOD. Then I bathed you with water, washed off your blood from you and anointed you with oil. I also clothed you with embroidered cloth and put sandals of porpoise skin on your feet; and I wrapped you with fine linen and covered you with silk. I adorned you with ornaments, put bracelets

on your hands and a necklace around your neck. I also put a ring in your nostril, earrings in your ears and a beautiful crown on your head. Thus you were adorned with gold and silver, and your dress was of fine linen, silk and embroidered cloth. You ate fine flour, honey and oil; so you were exceedingly beautiful and advanced to royalty. Then your fame went forth among the nations on account of your beauty, for it was perfect because of My splendor which I bestowed on you, declares the Lord GOD.

-Ezekiel 16:8-14

God waited until we were ready for love. He has always been ready for our relationship, but we have not. He waited for us, and then at the right time covered our nakedness. He covered all that made us ashamed, covering the exposed areas so that we could be in relationship. He covered us with robes of righteousness; not of our own, but Christ's. He made a covenant with us; and then, *You became MINE, declares the Lord* (v. 8).

Look at all the things He did for us AFTER we were His: He fed us. He clothed us in fine garments, adorned us with jewelry and covered our feet with shoes. A crown defined our royal identity. He bestowed on us His splendor, making our beauty even greater. What would be your response to God's actions? How would a wife respond to her husband who had made this overwhelming display of affection to her?

> *But you trusted in your beauty and played the harlot because of your fame, and you poured out your harlotries on every passerby who might be willing. You took some of your clothes, made for yourself high places of various colors and played the harlot on them, which should never come about nor happen. You also took your beautiful jewels made of My gold and of My silver, which I had given you, and made for yourself male images that you might play the harlot with them. Then you took your embroidered cloth and covered them, and offered My oil and My incense before them. Also My bread which I gave you, fine flour, oil and honey with which I fed you, you would offer before them for a soothing aroma; so it happened, declares the Lord GOD. Moreover, you took your sons and daughters whom you had borne to Me and sacrificed them to idols to be devoured. Were your harlotries so small a matter? You slaughtered My children and offered them up to idols by causing them to pass through the fire.*
>
> -Ezekiel 16:15-21

Probably not the reaction God was hoping for. And while we want to say we would never do this to

God, we do. We take the things God has given us and use them for our own selfish gain. Go back and read again how she took all the things God had given her and perverted them: She traded her beauty for harlotry. Her clothes became bedding, upon which she would entertain strangers. The beautiful jewels became objects to be worshiped. The bread, oil and incense that God had made for her delight became a gift to another. Then, as if the rest were not bad enough, she took the things that were born from the union between her and God—their children—and sacrificed them. She let the seed that God planted in her and enabled her to carry and give birth to pass through the fire (v. 21).

Do you see how "she," an image of God's people (you and me), abused God's extravagant gifts? When I say that Satan will use anything to entice you into his arms, I mean anything and everything. He will even take that speaking gift, that mercy gift, that encouragement gift and try to get you to use it against its original relationship- and kingdom-building purposes.

As God's people, we have to wake up and stop being so naïve. Make no mistake; the enemy is out to steal from you, kill you and destroy you (John 10:10). But ultimately, he has a whole world in mind; he needs to reproduce as well.

> *Therefore, my brethren, you also were made*
> *to die to the Law through the body of Christ,*

so that you might be joined to another, to Him who was raised from the dead, in order that we might bear fruit for God. For while we were in the flesh, the sinful passions, which were aroused by the Law, were at work in the members of our body to bear fruit for death.

-Romans 7:4-5

Have I made you uncomfortable enough yet? It's understandable that you don't want to think about carrying Satan's seed. But ignorance is not bliss; it's a tool of Satan's to get us to make choices that carry out his will and not God's. I understand that this is a hard picture, but you have to know what is true in order for you to know what is not.

We are capable of bearing fruit that leads to death. This battle between God's seed and Satan's started way before you and I were ever born—it began in the garden. Genesis 3:15 talks about the hatred that would exist between the woman's seed and Satan's; specifically, God is foretelling the birth of Christ through a woman, and the battle that would ensue between Him and Satan. What we haven't accepted yet is that because of our relationship with God, because He dwells within us, because we are one with Him, we are a part of that battle. Don't think that Satan won't try to get intimate with you in order to impregnate you with his ideals, his way of thinking, his subjective truths and his will.

It seemed I was pregnant with Satan's seed when I was in my sophomore year of college. It feels like one of those stories where a girl is pregnant and doesn't find out until she is about to give birth. When I look back at that time in my life, I can see all the pregnancy symptoms, but I reasoned them away. The battle for intimacy, for my identity, that I described is like looking through my pregnancy journal—only it wasn't God's seed I was carrying. How do I know? By what it eventually produced in my life. I was so wrapped up in finding someone or something to validate me that I never bothered to check the source of validation. I was preaching and teaching, leading small group Bible studies and I was chaplain of my dorm. At the same time, I was physically intimate with my boyfriend, trying to redefine what purity *really* was. I kept trying to draw closer to God, but there was something between us. I refused to let go of my pursuit of identity through people, even though God would beg me to leave the bed of His enemy. I did not trust Him enough. I had become one of those people that smiled, waved and kissed the babies with her husband while in public, but behind closed doors pursued filling a void by any means necessary. What birthed out of that season of my life was darkness and loneliness.

That's what a stranger's bed feels like: dark and lonely. Satan doesn't linger in bed with you. He doesn't wake you up with a smile on his face. He leaves you once he has gotten what he wants from you. He has used you, and now he is done.

"I have had sex with someone else." It's how honest we should be with God, but we rarely ever are. I don't tend to recognize my sins immediately because I don't think of them as "cheating on God." Don't claim it, right? Just rename it—that's the game we play. If we ever want to end the affair, we need to start by recognizing that we are having one. Now is the time to call it out. Otherwise you continue to live a lie, and no relationship flourishes in that environment. Pastor Robert Morris, pastor of one of the fastest growing churches in America says, "It's like slipping out of bed with God and committing adultery and then slipping back into bed with Him and hoping He doesn't notice." He notices. Our adultery hurts Him; it hurts us. When we call the sin out, we are confessing it. And while that is a start, God's ultimate desire is for us to repent.

Many people confess to God while still laying in a stranger's bed. You can recognize your sins, even confess them, and still do nothing about them. He wants you to get out of that stranger's bed and get back in bed with Him. We call that *repentance. Repent* comes from the Greek word *metanoia*, meaning a *change of mind*. Have you ever changed your mind? It usually happens when you see two choices clearly. That's what this chapter is all about: seeing that there are two beds you can lie in—Satan's or God's. Which bed have your choices led you to lie in?

It's okay to tell God the truth. He is the safest place for you to come to. While the world has tried to make you believe He is a harsh, cruel, tight-fisted, lightning-striking God, He is not. He is your Lover, and all He wants is for you to come home.

He isn't waiting for you to "get better" before He loves you; He already loves you. He will not love you any more or any less, no matter what might happen. Although we see all the dark places, God sees us as light and beautiful (Song of Solomon 1:5, 15; 2:1). He calls us fair even when we are standing in all of our dirt. He sees what you were made for. What often gets lost in marriage is this safe ground to be open and honest with each other. "Intimacy is the ability to love and be loved without the fear of rejection."[9] II Timothy 2:13 tells us that even though we are faithless, He remains faithful. He is still here for us; after all we have done, He remains. Listen to the end of that passage in Ezekiel:

> *All the same, I'll remember the covenant I made with you when you were young and I'll make a new covenant with you that will last forever. You'll remember your sorry past and be properly contrite when you receive back your sisters, both the older and the younger. I'll give them to you as daughters, but not as participants in your covenant. I'll firmly establish my covenant with you and you'll*

9   David Sunde

know that I am God. You'll remember your
past life and face the shame of it, but when
I make atonement for you, make everything
right after all you've done, it will leave you
speechless.

-Ezekiel 16:60-63

In His eyes, you have and always will be married to Him. Can a bride ever forget her wedding dress? (Jeremiah 2:32). Only if she never imagined herself married. I think that while God always sees the ring on His finger, we struggle to see ours.

In God's eyes, we are His. Over and over again in the Bible you see the possessive nature of God. He says these are "*My* people." His rage, seen throughout the Bible and especially in the Old Testament, is a jealous rage. God is our Husband and He does not deal kindly with those He finds us in bed with. God is a jealous God—and He wants us back in bed with Him. He is pursuing you.

I will give them a heart to know me, that I
am the Lord. **They will be my people, and**
I will be their God, *for they will return to me*
with all their heart.

-Jeremiah 24:7, NIV

'This is the covenant I will make with the
house of Israel after that time,' declares the
Lord. 'I will put my law in their minds and
write it on their hearts. **I will be their God,**

and they will be my people. '
-Jeremiah 31:33, NIV

They will be my people, and I will be their God.
-Jeremiah 32:38, NIV

Then they will follow my decrees and be careful to keep my laws. **They will be my people, and I will be their God.**
-Ezekiel 11:20, NIV

'Then the people of Israel will no longer stray from me, nor will they defile themselves anymore with all their sins. **They will be my people, and I will be their God,** *' declares the Sovereign Lord.*
-Ezekiel 14:11, NIV

They will no longer defile themselves with their idols and vile images or with any of their offenses, for I will save them from all their sinful backsliding, and I will cleanse them. **They will be my people, and I will be their God.**
-Ezekiel 37:23, NIV

My dwelling place will be with them; **I will be their God, and they will be my people.**
-Ezekiel 37:27, NIV

I will bring them back to live in Jerusalem; **they will be my people, and I will be faithful and righteous to them as their God.**
                                    -Zechariah 8:8, NIV

What agreement is there between the temple of God and idols? For we are the temple of the living God. As God has said: "I will live with them and walk among them, and **I will be their God, and they will be my people.***"*
                              -2 Corinthians, 6:16 NIV

This is the covenant I will make with the house of Israel after that time, declares the Lord. I will put my laws in their minds and write them on their hearts. **I will be their God, and they will be my people***.*
                              -Hebrews 8:10, NIV

Are you starting to get it? Do you see how in love God is with you? Look around; where have your choices left you? What do you need to say to God right now? When are you going to talk about what's really going on in your relationship with Him? Today? It doesn't matter how long it's been; He still loves you. He is committed to you, and He wants you back.

chapter eight | **pain**

My wedding night was rough; it wasn't the fairy tale we hear about. I don't believe that I am alone in this experience; but on that night I believed myself to be the only woman to have cried for her new groom.

To put it mildly, there is pain in intimacy.

No one talks about this much to a bride before her wedding night. It's like everyone knows it's a possibility, but no one wants to be the one to tell her. There seems to be an unwritten vow of secrecy that every married woman takes. (The same vow will be required regarding pregnancy and birth; no one will give the mom-to-be the real details.) She may ask, but people will avoid the question.

People will buy gifts for the couple's home. The bride's thoughts will be consumed about flowers and shoe sizes. Nothing, not even her bridesmaids' lingerie party, will hint at what's ahead. Even her fiancée is in on this hoax.

When you enter into a marriage, people wisely tell you to seek counsel first. If you live in North America, though, that can mean very little. Most pastors and counselors are not bold enough to tell two individuals not to marry. And on the off chance that they are bold enough, engaged couples have often shut off their ability to reason, so they reject the counsel.

But let's imagine a world where things actually work as they are supposed to: let's imagine that before two people get engaged they seek some counseling. In this time with their counselor they cover issues like finances, goals, dreams, personality types, moral beliefs, children, commitment … you know, all the important stuff. At the end of their time together, the counselor gives his or her advice and the two are left with a decision to make: to move forward together, or part ways. That sounds good—so reasonable, and void of the true emotions involved.

Why does no one offer pre-marital counseling before we enter into our marriage with God? We could have a chance to express our expectations and dreams. What we fear could be laid on the table. Finances could be discussed; we could find out that God wants us to trust Him with the first fruits of our money and not the last. God could show us His law, His authority, but from His heart, and how it's written on ours. What about children? We would find out that God wants to reproduce His love, dreams and talents in us. And most importantly, we would find out that it could hurt to be with God.

Recently, I heard a sermon by Erwin McManus that talked about this.[10] It was the first time that I had ever really had to grapple with this concept. We can be right in the center of God's will and be in pain, or unsafe, or even about to die. Yes, I knew life wasn't easy; but yet, in a way, this realization was freeing for me. No longer did I have to seek a life where everything seemed neat and orderly. I didn't have to try and explain why this hard thing was happening to me. McManus pointed out that the very person who was connected with Jesus best on earth, John the Baptist, was beheaded—and Jesus allowed it.

I realized that my definition of peace was all wrong. *Peace* is not the same as *safety*. When God promised us peace, He never said that it always meant you would be *safe*. That is why He promises us the peace that surpasses all understanding (Philippians 4:7). So while there may be pain in intimacy, there is still peace. A peace that pulls me through the pain to the other side. A peace that says I don't get it, but God does. A peace that reminds you that you are not alone.

There is pain in intimacy.

It can hurt to be with God. While all pain does not originate with God, He can handle any we might

---

10   McManus, Erwin. *The Barbaric Way Out of Civilization*. Sermon.

(Romans 8:28). In the beginning, it can seem pointless, but He can use that pain to lead you to more—of you, and of Him. More of who God designed you to be. More of what God empowered you to be able to do.

More, more, more.

This pain is more like physical exercise than physical intimacy. God wants to be your Lover and your Coach. (My husband has no problem filling both of those roles.) Let's admit it; we are flabby in some areas. I don't just mean physically, but spiritually. There are places in our spiritual lives that we have allowed to feed and continue feeding without taking the time to exercise our faith. We know *about* things, we've heard them preached on, we've read a book on it—and yet we act on nothing. We plop on our spiritual couches and apathetically watch life pass us by. Being honest hurts. Letting the one who has seen you naked tell you what you need to work on is hard. But who do you want to push you—someone who knows you inside and out and loves you anyway, or a stranger? We've been choosing the stranger for far too long. Let your Lover talk to you.

There is pain in intimacy.

Part of your journey with God will hurt. Paul writes to the Corinthians about his own journey through intimacy and pain.

[I have been] … In far more labors, in far more imprisonments, beaten times without number, often in danger of death. Five times I received from the Jews thirty-nine lashes. Three times I was beaten with rods, once I was stoned, three times I was shipwrecked, a night and a day I have spent in the deep. I have been on frequent journeys, in dangers from rivers, dangers from robbers, dangers from my countrymen, dangers from the Gentiles, dangers from in the city, dangers from in the wilderness, dangers on the sea, dangers among false brethren; I have been in labor and hardship, through many sleepless nights, in hunger and thirst, often without food, in cold and exposure.

-II Corinthians 11:23b-27

If anyone sought after intimacy with God, it was Paul—and these are what Paul's footsteps of pain looked like. Paul forsook marriage in order to fully understand that intimacy. And yet we want what Paul had with God, without any of the dangers.

Paul isn't the only one who hurt because of who he chose to love. David was anointed as a king at a young age; but, for his Lover, he faced the possibility of death against a barbaric warrior. He had spears thrown at him by the king, and he spent the better part of his young adult life on the run.

Think about Esther. While we may think that a

year of beauty treatments was a plush assignment from God, it was not. Esther did not choose to go to the palace to be paraded in a beauty contest. She avoided it; but after four years of searching had produced no results, the officials were sent to find eligible women. Even though Esther passed through the first round of the eligible queen contest, she still only asked for the minimum treatments to be applied to her. She did not want to be chosen. King Ahasuerus was not Jewish, and he openly hated the Jews. In the palace, Esther was in exile; away from what she knew and unable to openly worship the God she loved. Marrying the king was not a love story; it was an invitation to be a part of a harem. She was being sold into slavery. Do you really think she could have told the king "not tonight"? This was not an easy place; it was horrible, it was hard and it was painful.

These are people that we admire and even aspire to be like, but we tend to ignore the painful parts of their stories. We believe in a theology that is not in the Bible. We believe in a spiritual umbrella of God's protection. Does God protect us? Yes. But the way we have always viewed that umbrella is as protection against pain, just like an umbrella doesn't let you get wet.

The truth is, you are going to get wet in this journey. The difference that God brings is the hand that holds yours in the rain. We don't walk through pain and tragedies alone. Who can protect you better than the one who is in the midst of the storm with you?

It's time to fight for your marriage with Him, because everything in this world is fighting against it.

I don't want some vague umbrella hovering above me in the midst of my storms; I want someone beside me, stepping in the puddles, lifting me up, even helping me sing in the rain.

There is pain in intimacy.

When you get married, no one tells you that this will be the hardest thing you will ever do. There is no card that tells you to remember to keep pushing through the hard times, to stick by each other when it hurts, to love when it's easier to hate, to fight to keep your marriage together. But the reality is all of that—and more. Sure, you can have an existence with God that never grows, never appears to hurt, and can be used by you at anytime; but that's not a marriage, that's a gumball machine. You want more? So does God. It's time to fight for your marriage with Him, because everything in this world is fighting against it. Satan has made sure of that.

There is pain in intimacy.

I believe those who have gone through the deepest tragedies have had the opportunity to know God in some of the most intimate ways. I am not saying that you can't know God apart from tragedy, but I am saying that there is a unique intimacy that exists between God and His lover in the midst of pain. I just read the blog of a woman my age who lost her daughter at three months, and then two years later her husband became a quadriplegic from a scuba accident. Reading her story was like the tree mentioned in Psalm 91:3: her roots were deep.

This is the area that we don't want to have to face in our faith. Many things cause pain: Satan's attack, the consequence of my sins, the choices of others, or just the result of living in a fallen world. But I can't always blame those things and avoid the hard gaze of pain that our Lover may allow in our lives.

There is pain in intimacy.

Perhaps this is the place in our relationship with God where He takes on more of a fatherly tone. Or maybe that is how we like to see Him so that it makes sense. We have seen, experienced or contributed to the role of a parent who allows something hard to happen to their children in order for them to learn a lesson. It is often justified by the thought that "it was the only way they were going to learn." But to revert to that image for my Lover is to do just that—revert. Seeing God as our Father is not a step back, but making all of His actions fatherly is. And just because I can't see my spouse doing this to me doesn't mean it can't be true of God. *My Lover purposely and purposefully allowed me to be in a painful situation.* Sounds like a statement said before a divorce court judge. At times, God allows pain to enter into our lives. But is it really just to learn a lesson? Yes and no. Yes, there is a lesson to gain, but no, because the lesson is not the summation of the painful circumstance.

It's all about our relationship. What makes a strong marriage is not that you stuck it out through the sunny days, but through the rainy ones too. You got wet together, muddy together, tanned together, sore together, bitten together, tired together, _____ together ... do you see the operative word here? *Together!* It's not fun and you don't see the full results until the end, but in your togetherness, your oneness is revealed. That's intimate.

There is pain in intimacy.

If you want true intimacy, true relationship, then begin to embrace the painful situations. Fearing those situations only puts something between you and God. You know the feeling. You're talking with someone you are close with, but there is something in the air or in the way he is talking to you. *Is it him or me?* you wonder. When it's between you and God—it's you. Your Lover wants to meet you at every high and low place you walk. He doesn't watch from above, He watches from beside you. Can you feel Him right now? He is next to you as you read. He doesn't need a worship song, a Bible or a sermon. He enjoys your presence and longs for you to enjoy His.

Pain makes you think. Pain is both reflective and revealing; it causes you to reflect deeply about who you are and who you believe God is. How can you be intimate with someone you have only believed part of the truth about? How can you let God love you when you have only been halfway honest with Him?

Do I need to say it again? There is pain in intimacy.

Most of all, pain makes you *move*. First by making you squirm, but then by making you look around for some kind of way out. Is this where I am supposed to be? Am I doing something wrong? Is there something else I am supposed to be doing? Think about the story of Joseph in the Bible. Not the part where he has great dreams about all God wanted to do with him. Not the part where he is his dad's favorite kid. You know, the part where he is sold into slavery—the part that landed him in Potiphar's house. It was bad at first, but then Joseph made the most of his situation. He's in a horribly painful situation, and yet the dialogue between him and God is still intimate.

Was Potiphar's house God's ultimate for Joseph? No. Joseph did nothing wrong in that situation. He had worked hard and become the head of Potiphar's house. Joseph didn't love where he was, but it started to get a little comfortable. He was the head of the house. At this point, he remembered the dreams God put on his heart, but they started to seem a little distant. Imagine the conversations Joseph must have had with God, while abandoned in a hole or sitting in a jail. "Why, God?" Could God have taken him straight from Jesse's house to Pharaoh's? Yes. But what the enemy intended for evil, God intended for good (Genesis 50:20). While sometimes it looks like your enemy is winning, God has already won that battle. And He sees those that come against you; they are not bigger than His plans.

What does your pain say about how you see your Lover? To ignore this question is to say to God, "I'm okay if we just keep our relationship the way it is; no more, no less." Talk to Him. If the pain reveals some hard things about yourself and some ungodly views about Him, tell Him. He doesn't want a relationship that is neat and superficial, He wants a real one—with disappointments, tears, joy, laughter, questions and doubts. A real relationship is the only way you can be truly intimate with God. A real relationship means you have to talk to your Lover more, include Him in your journey more, think about Him more, hang with Him more … more. If you want more in your relationship with Him, then let Him into more of your life. How about into all of it?

Pain moves you. It pushes you out of your comfort zone and into a fork in the road; you have a choice.

There *is* pain in intimacy. Where will you allow your pain to take you?

chapter nine |**destiny**

Your future will happen, but your destiny doesn't have to. It doesn't depend on your behavior; but the more intimate you are with God, the more you become the person He designed you to be. Your destiny is a matter of who you are—your identity. What you will become flows directly from that source. It is not an arrival point, it is a journey; take it one choice at a time.

When you marry, it's an agreement to both the present and the future; you don't marry someone just to enjoy the moment. The present is what you see, what you know, what you are experiencing. But almost everyone believes in a better future, where our dreams are alive and walking, where things are easier (where you're ten pounds thinner and really toned).

But what if I told you that someone else has been thinking about your future? What if I told you that they think about it more than you do? And what if that someone has a plan for it? You would want to meet them, right? You would want to ask them questions and drill them for every detail. Part of our relationship with God is based on the belief that we have a great future with Him. That's good, but He has more than that for you. Have you trusted Him for more—to take you past your future to your destiny?

It's easier to believe in a future than in a destiny. The future is going to happen; nothing can stop that. But your destiny doesn't have to happen. Let that sink in for a moment. *Your destiny does not have to happen.* We assume it will happen, but that is a poor assumption. The choices you make are either walking you in the direction of your destiny or on the road away from it. I used to believe that the longer I lived, the closer I would be to my destiny.

You can be 90 years old and just as far from your destiny as you were at 35. Pastor Robert Morris says it this way: "No one can thwart the destiny on your life except you."[11] Proverbs says, *People ruin their lives by their own foolishness and then are angry at the LORD* (Proverbs 19:3, NLT). It's your destiny. They're your choices.

Your life has a very specific destiny, although we tend to believe that we have a generic destiny as Christians: we are going to grow in God, He is going to bless us, and we are going to use our generic gifts to build His kingdom. And that is what we settle for: a generic destiny.

11   Pastor Robert Morris, Gateway Church. Southlake, Texas.

Paulo Coelho in his book *The Alchemist* says that we each have a "personal legend," and that legend is under our direction. We can manage it or we can relinquish it. Our relinquishment, he says, is most often to "the world's greatest lie."

> "'What's the world's greatest lie?' the boy asked, completely surprised. 'It's this: that at a certain point in our lives, we lose control of what's happening to us, and our lives become controlled by fate. That's the world's greatest lie.'"[12]

Only generic gods make generic destinies. That's the only way it can work. To be a God that is specific, timely, challenging, real and authentic, you would have to be alive—and only one God is alive. God desires to share the plan with you. He didn't create you in order for you to learn to be independent from Him. The long talks, the silence, the good days, the bad … the journey is what He had in mind, not just one decision. It's the whole process and not just one moment that He looks forward to. You have a destiny. And it's not something that is just out there in the future, but right here and right now.

One of the greatest inhibitors to our destiny is fear. I think if God showed us His full plan for our lives the way we might view a film, we would be afraid.

---

12   Coelho, Paulo. *The Alchemist*. New York: HarperCollins, 2006. 18. Print.

Sure, we would be excited at first, but then fear would beset us; we might think, "How am I going to make that happen?" And then, as all good Christians do, we say, "Oh no, that's God's job." But inside the wheels would keep turning, wouldn't they? "I need to learn this, I need to go there. I need to meet this person. I need to read this book." We would get to work, not allowing God to be the one who molds and shapes us.

Sometimes we feel inspired by God: He gives us a glimpse of His blueprint for us, and then we take it and make it our own. We plan it out, we form it around our lives, we tell others, and then we assume that all of life's events are pointing toward it. The only time we realize that we believe in a pseudo-God-designed destiny is when something goes wrong. So we take our partially envisioned destiny and human-size it. We break it up into manageable pieces. No God needed. But no matter how much you do, you can never fulfill your destiny by yourself. And that scares us.

Dr. Gary Smalley writes about the fears we bring into our relationships and our reactions to them. We fear rejection, judgment, disconnection, loneliness, failure, powerlessness, being invalidated, unhappiness, inferiority, being misunderstood, worthlessness and more.[13] What about you? What fears do you bring to your marriage with God? Are you afraid that if you release your destiny into His hands, you will end up in a place you don't love with people you hardly like? Do you fear He might plan a destiny where you will fail?

13   Smalley, Dr. Gary. Ibid. 27. Print.

If you relinquish your control, are you afraid you'll just be a puppet for God?

What most of us have been missing in our relationship with Him is honesty; let's be real with Him. Don't be afraid to ask questions. He wants to hear every thought, fear and emotion you have; He's the safest place for all of that. But we don't think that way, do we? The safest place in our minds is a friend, or ourselves; even the barber seems safer. If God is still that unapproachable deity with a lightning rod, then you have not gotten to know Him at all.

> *Ask and it will be given to you; seek and you will find; knock and the door will be opened to you. For everyone who asks receives; he who seeks finds; and to him who knocks, the door will be opened. Which of you, if his son asks for bread, will give him a stone? Or if he asks for a fish, will give him a snake? If you, then, though you are evil, know how to give good gifts to your children, how much more will your Father in heaven give good gifts to those who ask him!*
> -Matthew 7:7-11

God is trying to get you to look at Him differently. In the passage above in Matthew, Jesus talks about one view of Him, as a Father. How much better is God as a Father than the ones we've seen? Take the greatest marriage relationship you have seen, or maybe just imagined. On their best behavior, they still fall short. How much better is God as a spouse than any of the ones you've seen?

Let Him be so much more in your life. You were made for more, but are you experiencing it? He only wants to give good gifts to you. Fear is a choice. Remember, "no one can thwart the destiny on your life except you."[14] If you believe God to be unsafe, judgmental, *only* a friend or *only* your Savior, then you will always live in some aspect of fear when you're in His presence.

In *The Chronicles of Narnia*, C.S. Lewis writes of a lion named Aslan as a metaphor for God. The children, Peter, Susan, Edmund and Lucy, each have a unique reaction to their encounter with Him.

"At the name of Aslan each one of the children felt something jump in its inside. Edmund felt a sensation of mysterious horror. Peter felt suddenly brave and adventurous. Susan felt as if some delicious smell or some delightful strain of music had just floated by her. And Lucy got the feeling you have when you wake up in the morning and realize that it is the beginning of the holidays or the beginning of summer."[15]

---

14   Pastor Robert Morris, Gateway Church. Southlake, Texas.
15   Lewis, C.S. *The Chronices of Narnia: The Lion, the Witch, and the Wardrobe.* New York: HarperTrophy, 1950. 68. Print.

We each respond to God according to what we truly believe about Him. God has a destiny for your life, both for now and in the future. Don't let fear come between you. Our true destinies must be larger then ourselves; otherwise it is just a goal. We know about goals: we set them, we think through them ... we break them up into achievable tasks. But I can achieve my goals without God. God wanted you to need Him. He wants you to include Him in reaching your destiny, so He made it impossible to reach it without Him.

Spouses understand each other; at least the good ones do. Your spouse has been around you enough to know what you are thinking and why you just said what you just said. God understands you. He knows you better than you know yourself. In fact, His own words to you in Psalm 139:3 say that He is *intimately acquainted with all your ways*. He doesn't have to intimately know our ways. He could choose not to. But He didn't. He chose to *know* you, to knit you together, to number the hairs on your head. And in some amazing, unfathomable way, He makes each of us feel like we are the only one who has such a close relationship with Him, even though we know it's available for all of us.

Our relationships with God, like our destinies, are not contained in a bubble. They both involve other people. There have been people that have invested in my marriage and people that have tried to tear it apart. But Remember Henri Nouwen's thought that our chosen-ness was not at the exclusion of others, but the inclusion of them. God has purposed His people, His church, to better the relationship we have with Him. Each day we go to church is like couple's therapy, and each week that follows is our platform to practice what we have learned. People will enhance or destroy your relationship with God, and both motives can be used to make your marriage with Him better.

I have some friendships that encourage my marriage with God, and even inspire me to become more creative in it. But some friendships are like "Debbie-Downers." As much as you try and stay encouraged in what you're in the midst of, they point to any negative reality they can find. Those intimate experiences in your relationship with God that were harvested from the harsh grains of sand in life have produced a pearl—but be careful not to throw your pearls to the pigs (Matthew 7:6).

Take this book for instance. Some friends I have spoken to have encouraged and inspired me as I have written it. And yet, without realizing it, some have discouraged it greatly. The pages of this book are filled with many pearls that my Lover has strung together and placed on my neck. Had I listened to some, my neck would be left empty, with no evidence of my encounters with Him.

But people not only aid or hinder our relationship, they can aid or hinder our destiny as well. We cannot achieve our destinies alone. That does not mean that we cannot fulfill them apart from God; that means that we cannot fulfill them apart from other people.

He has designed us so that as we grow closer to Him, we will reach our hands out to others: to our friends, our family and our neighbors. Then our eyes are opened to seeing those we don't like, those we don't want to touch or be near, the *least of these* (Matthew 25:40). This way, more people have an opportunity to draw near to Him; everyone gets a chance to know Him. And who better to introduce someone to Him than His bride?

Remember what Jesus said to the teacher who was asking what the most important commandment was: *Love the Lord your God with all your heart and with all your soul and with all your mind and with all your strength.' The second is this: 'Love your neighbor as yourself.' There is no commandment greater than these* (Mark 12:30-31). Start with your relationship with Him, but don't stay there. Everything comes full circle to our intimacy with God. It is always affecting, and being affected. You will inspire others to draw near to Him and other people will inspire you to do the same.

But it is wise to be aware that Satan uses people as well. Satan would like nothing more than to diminish your destiny. He fears you fulfilling it, and he is using everything in his power to come against it. Have you ever heard of the theory of osmosis? (Biology major I am not, but this I actually remember.) You have two areas: one that is highly concentrated, the other, not so much. As these two areas stay in contact long enough, the result is an even concentration between the two areas as one bleeds into the other. Your mother wasn't lying; we really do become like the people we are around. And if the people around us are believers in small destinies … eventually, you will be too.

People can cause us to settle for less. Or sometimes we feel bad for other people because we have found such fulfillment in finding our true destiny. And so we scale back a bit, so as to not offend or hurt them.

Another way we diminish our destinies is that we ask people to fulfill our destiny for us. We ask our friends, mentors, pastors and spouses to be everything for us, to do what we know God has called us to do. It's easier if someone else handles the pain, the fear, the hard parts. We prefer our comfort zones.

Sometimes we try and copy someone else's journey. We haven't allowed God to speak to our hearts about our own true and unique destiny, but we see the life and passion in someone who has; and so we think that if we just do what they're doing, we will find that same joy and passion. But that is not the means God uses. It can be a spark; we all have heroes, and mentors are a crucial part of our journey. But others cannot be the main source of our destiny. God has a specific plan, a blueprint, in mind for you. He crafts those plans individually and reveals them intimately—not in mass production.

With intimacy comes the probability of reproduction. The more frequent the connection, the greater probability of conception. What you co-create

God has a specific plan, a blueprint, in mind for you.

He crafts them individually and reveals them intimately—not in mass production.

with God is a part of your destiny. Know this: God is not after your connection simply for reproduction. He loves you for you.

But as you draw closer to God you become aware of the possibility of conception; you're not really surprised by it. In fact, the closer you grow to your Husband, the more you welcome it, even plan for it. With your permission comes conception—moving you from a future to a destiny. And with conception, you walk out the process of carrying that co-creation inside of you. Finally, you will arrive at the point where you find yourself giving birth to those things that you and God have conceived together. You couldn't (nor would you want to) stay pregnant with those passionate desires and burdens forever.

All around us we observe a pregnant creation. The difficult times of pain throughout the world are simply birth pangs. But it's not only around us; it's within us. The Spirit of God is arousing us within. We're also feeling the birth pangs. These sterile and barren bodies of ours are yearning for full deliverance. That is why waiting does not diminish us, any more than waiting diminishes a pregnant mother. We are enlarged in the waiting. We, of course, don't see what is enlarging us. But the longer we wait, the larger we become, and the more joyful our expectancy.
-Romans 8:22-25, MSG

We believe our destiny is on hold while we wait. But your waiting does not *diminish* you; your destiny did not stop because you had kids, or lost your job or went unnoticed by your boss. When you are pregnant, the waiting enlarges you. But one day you will deliver; that day is part of your destiny too.

At that point, you will have a daily responsibility for it. It no longer remains as a dream or idea but a reality. Being married to God means taking care of those things that you have birthed out of your intimacy with Him. Are there things already born that you haven't taken care of? Maybe you have a heart for the homeless, or the elderly or for the environment. Maybe it's for fitness, or helping finance God's kingdom work on this Earth. There is something that God is stirring in you that He desires for you to carry, birth and nurture. Are you taking care of it? He gave you the tools to do it. Don't be afraid of your destiny—the one now or in the future. God has prepared you for it; your giftings are what He gave you to nurture what you've birthed.

Now there are varieties of gifts, but the same Spirit. And there are varieties of ministries, and the same Lord. There are varieties of effects, but the same God who works all things in all persons. But to each one is given the manifestation of the Spirit for the common good. For to one is given the word of wisdom through the Spirit, and to another the word of knowledge according to the same Spirit; to another faith by the same Spirit, and to another gifts of healing by the one Spirit, and to another the effecting of miracles, and to another prophecy, and to another the distinguishing of spirits, to another various kinds of tongues, and to another the interpretation of tongues. But one and the same Spirit works all these things, distributing to each one individually just as He wills.

-I Corinthians 12:4-11

There are also the gifts of teaching, preaching, serving, leadership, pastoring, evangelism, mercy, encouragement, administration and giving.[16] He knew what you needed to raise this child. It's one thing to be faithful to God conceiving those passions and dreams within you; it's another thing to actually take personal, daily responsibility for it. Your destiny is not just a lofty idea—it is a reality for you to live, starting now.

The children I have require a lot, and they're not even hard kids. I can't choose to not take care of them on any given day; well, I could, but I wouldn't have them for long. What I choose to do, or not do, directly affects them. I have a responsibility to them on my good days and my bad ones, when I feel like it and when I wish I could multiply myself, just to get it all done.

---

16   I Corinthians 12, 14; Romans 12; Ephesians 4

Daily means every day, not just when the timing is right, or convenient, or the most beneficial to you. Are you stewarding what He has shown you about your destiny? Kenneth often asks me how the kids are doing today—what we did, what was hard, what they said. God wants to talk to you about the very thing the two of you created together. How they are today, and what they will become in the future.

After 9,855 days of believing in a greater destiny than he was experiencing, Nelson Mandela eventually became the first South African president to be elected democratically. In 1962 he was arrested and wrongly convicted of sabotage and other charges, and sentenced to life in prison. Mandela served the next 27 years behind bars, but he never gave up on his destiny. He worked to free people from hopeless circumstances and mindsets. Marianne Williamson captures much of what Mandela stands for with her powerful words; rooted in truth, and the belief that there is more for each of us:

> *Our deepest fear is not that we are inadequate. Our deepest fear is that we are powerful beyond measure. It is our light, not our darkness that most frightens us. We ask ourselves, Who am I to be brilliant, gorgeous, talented, fabulous? Actually, who are you not to be? You are a child of God. Your playing small does not serve the world. There is nothing enlightened about shrinking*

so that other people won't feel insecure around you. We are all meant to shine, as children do. We were born to make manifest the glory of God that is within us. It's not just in some of us; it's in everyone. And as we let our own light shine, we unconsciously give other people permission to do the same. As we are liberated from our own fear, our presence automatically liberates others.[17]

In our society, we work in order to ensure our future. In God's economy, His work has already secured our destiny. No longer are you limited to gleaning the corners of the field, you now own the field. *'In that day,' declares the Lord, 'you will call me "my husband;" you will no longer call me "my master"'* (Hosea 2:16).

It all starts with you and your Husband. Talk to Him; really talk to Him. Ask Him about your destiny and the future children you will create together. Open up the conversation, begin the dialogue. He has so much to share with you. Let intimacy show you your destiny. Don't just wait for it to happen.

---

17   Williamson, Marianne. *A Return to Love: Reflections on the Principles of a Course in Miracles.* New York City: Harper Collins, 1992. Print.

chapter ten | **marriage**

God's vows to you:

I take you, as My friend, My love,
*   and My beloved wife,*
*   loving you now and as you grow*
*   and develop into all that I see budding in you.*
I vow to be faithful to you,
*   even in times when you are faithless.*
I will love you when our lives are at peace
*   and when they are in turmoil;*
*   when I hear your words of love toward me*
*   and when I am hurt by you; in times of rest*
*   and in times of work.*
When you are spiritually sick
*   and when you are healthy.*
I will honor and respect your goals and dreams
*   and help you to fulfill them.*
From the depth of My being,
*   I will seek to be open and honest with you.*

I will laugh with you and cry with you,
and promise to cherish you
for as long as we both shall eternally live.
I vow these things knowing
that My unwavering nature and love
is in the midst of it all.

So what does it look like to be married to God? No, I mean after the vows, after the honeymoon, when the "feelings" wear away and I am left with the reality of my day. You know, the one with alarm clocks, meetings, car lines, television and dinner plans. When I can't remember all the details like I used to about our wedding, and the bridesmaids have long ago donated their dresses to charity.

I have made much of the bedroom between you and God. That was intentional. But some people want to live in the bedroom and never get up and go to work. Is it either/or? Can one have both? The truth is that the passion and connection that happens in the bedroom is a sustainer and motivator for life. It's like the wink over coffee the next morning.

There isn't just one way to have a marriage, but there are some fundamentals to a good marriage. There are ways to talk that get you into fights (I have a list) and ways to talk that draw you near to each other. There is a mentality that says I make choices with us in mind, and one that says I was only thinking about *me*.

Nothing affects your decision-making like being

married. You may have a close friend, but you don't consult him when you want to buy your groceries. Your mother has only so many opinions you can consider. But a marriage, a good one, always affects your choices. You begin to ask questions like, "Do we have enough money in the budget to eat out for lunch today?", "Should I talk to this person?," or "Should I go to this place?"

God makes decisions with you in mind. He cares about all of you, not because He is tallying a record of your choices, hoping the good outweigh the bad. You aren't under a spiritual microscope with your every move being dissected. You are His wife. He loves you more than you will ever love Him. He thinks about you all the time.

Many people don't often consider their spouse when making decisions. It's a weird switch to go from thinking independently to thinking about two people, especially when you can't see your partner with your physical eyes.

I am constantly asking Kenneth how things are going between us. How was the meal, are we talking enough (am I talking too much), is there anything I can do better, is the bedroom still great? You laugh, but I don't want to know things are going wrong by one of us ending up in bed with someone else—physically or mentally. And neither does God. We need to seek Him to reveal where we have allowed the enemy to gain a foothold or let a hard situation become another bed to lay in.

All of us need to ask God how our relationship is. And are there things you need to be honest with God about as well—your frustrations, your disappointments? He wants to know. Which brings up another area that seems to go untouched in real life: disappointment.

When you encounter disappointment, it is a reaction to an unmet expectation. As humans, whether we vocalize it or not, we expect things. And in marriage, for better or for worse, we expect a lot. Many husbands expect their wives to be like their mothers, and wives expect their husbands to be like their fathers. Unless, of course, you don't like your mother or father and you expect your spouse to be the opposite of them. See, expectations. They are there, but the question is, do you see them? And if you see them, are you willing to be honest enough with your spouse to admit them?

With God, when you encounter a disappointment, you talk to Him about it. You don't cover it up and suppress the underlying expectation. You talk. Sounds novel, I know. But honesty (spoken in love) is the real start to learning how to communicate with your spouse. Instead of starting a conversation about what you think He needs to fix, or how He can do better at something, start with you. What do you need to admit? Where are you disappointed? What are your unmet expectations? Then watch as God answers your deepest fears and disappointments. You do believe that God, your Lover, is bigger than those things, right?

To no surprise, communication is one of the main causes of divorce. It has a fancier name in court— irreconcilable differences. But at its base level, it's a communication problem. You have a method of communication, you like it, it obviously works for you; but you're not the only one in this relationship. Two have become one. So now you don't just have to understand how *you* communicate, but how *He* communicates too.

How have you been showing God love? How do you need to receive His? Don't limit how you love God. And don't limit how God can love you. People communicate love differently; some with words of affirmation, others with quality time. They could express it through receiving gifts, acts of service, or physical touch.[18] Drawing close to God is the best way to learn about how both of you speak love. You are humans, not textbooks; begin face-to-face.

In Numbers 12:7-8 we find God describing His intimate communication with Moses. *With him I speak mouth to mouth, even openly, and not in dark sayings, and he beholds the form of the Lord.* God wants to speak with you. He doesn't want to leave a voicemail or text you. He wants to meet with you personally, to be closer to you.

May he kiss me with the kisses of his mouth! (Song of Solomon 1:2a).

---

18   Chapman, Gary. *The Five Love Languages.* Chicago: Northfield, 1992. Print

He literally wants to pour the words out of His mouth and into yours. Don't get caught up in an earthly vision of a kiss here. Think of what a kiss means. It's purposeful, you have to be close to receive it, God looks at you (really sees you) and still wants to be close to you. Why? So you can be His puppet? No, because He loves you. His Words are the kisses you need for your day. They are given in the Bible, but they are also waiting for you all through your day. Your Husband is alive and walking next to you every 24 hours you are given. When Jesus left, He promised someone greater than Himself to come live inside us—the Holy Spirit. You can hear His Word, His kiss; but will you acknowledge it as that?

That stoplight you needed to make to be on time to your meeting … *A kiss.*

Your favorite soup of the day being served on the wrong day … *A kiss.*

The idea you came up with for a proposal you had to give your boss … *A kiss.*

What you read in the Bible is being preached about on Sunday … *A kiss.*

His kiss can be simple and it can be deep. When Kenneth would go away on a business trip, I would tuck little love letters to him inside his suitcase for him to find every morning. I wanted him to know as he walked into his day that he was loved, valued and missed. If I, being human, would want to do this for my husband, how much more does God leave a trail of His Words, His kisses for us to find each day?

Life's demands will always be infinitely longer than the finite time you have been given. Make the time to be intimate with God. In the natural world, the bedroom can easily get lost in the daily grind. If a couple is not intentional about it, the day will end and both parties will be disappointed, knowingly or not. But God designed us with a need for the bedroom. He longs for you to see that need as well. So, get intentional. Create a holy anticipation for your time with your Husband. Jeremiah 2:2 talks about God reminiscing about the devotion of their youth and *how as a bride you loved me* (NIV). Many jokes are made about newlyweds and their time spent in the bedroom. If your marriage is healthy, the bedroom only gets better—if you make room for it.

The bedroom should bring pleasure, not duty. If you are feeling more duty in your times with God, then change it up. Stop trying to be intimate with Him in the same position. Get out of the house, go to the park, take a walk around the neighborhood—do something different. There is an enemy out there and he loves to use your common, safe, predictable routine with God to get you bored, uninterested and unfulfilled by your relationship with Him.

Your marriage with God should be just that: your marriage. It should be tailored around your personality, your temperament, your loves and desires. I love to get creative with God.

I have written poetry to God.

I have water-colored the book of Isaiah.
> (My Crayola watercolor ran out of red; lots of blood in that book.)

I have rewritten Psalm 119 in my own words.

I have had a lunch date with Him.

I have taken pictures to capture what I read in a verse.

I have sketched a picture God showed me.

I have danced before God.

I have Googled more things than I should have to understand His Word.

I have given up television to spend more time talking to God.

I have taken a day alone with God in the park, on the side of a mountain, down by the river.

You can try something new with God that will keep your relationship fresh and new. The list above is not a recommendation but an inspiration. Feel free to think outside the box. Get off of the ladder. It's not about rungs; it's about your relationship. There is nothing that saddens God's heart more than when we sit before Him in our "quiet times" out of duty, and "hurry up and get this over with." Why don't you

Your marriage with God is
no͡t about an arrival point.

just tell Him you have a headache? Be real with Him. *Draw near to God and He will draw near to you* (James 4:8). That's a promise.

Do you like sunrise? I don't like the time they occur, but I sure do love the ones I get up to see. They are kind of a funny thing to watch. If the weather forecaster says the sunrise will occur at 6:15 am, don't be saddened that it isn't there when you first sit down to watch. It doesn't happen immediately; it's a process. Five minutes go by, you see a little more of the sunrise. Another ten and you are becoming pleased at what you see. Fifteen and you are smiling at this beautiful gift in front of you. Half an hour passes and you are in awe. But at what point did you see the sunrise? All of them. When we think of a sunrise, we often think of the finale. But every moment out there is a part of the sunrise. Our culture has influenced us to be creatures of destinations. We like arriving. Getting to places. The finish line. You will spend more of your life in process than at destinations. Learn to love the journey.

Your marriage with God is not about an arrival point. You aren't racing somebody to the finish. Like the sunrise, it's a process, it can keep getting better and better. Don't be discouraged if you are sitting there looking at the horizon, thinking, "This is it?" Stay awhile. It's just the beginning. Allow Him to come alongside you, take your hand and walk with you. The view only gets better.

I'm not saying that I have this all together, that I have it made. But I am well on my way, reaching out for Christ, who has so wondrously reached out for me. Friends, don't get me wrong: By no means do I count myself an expert in all of this, but I've got my eye on the goal, where God is beckoning us onward - to Jesus. I'm off and running, and I'm not turning back.

-Philippians 3:12-14, MSG

chapter eleven | **the end?**

And now I pronounce you …

So here we are. The last chapter. The one that we hope sums it all up, giving you the handbook as you close its pages. But marriages do not come with handbooks. Many couples wish they would, but spouses couldn't even write a handbook on themselves, let alone their partner. And while God's Word provides an amazing parameter for us to walk out our married life in, it's still YOUR journey with God. You have to make the choice and move from these black and white pages to a full-color reality.

Here's the truth. Being married to God is not something you do; it's who you are. You are married. You can stay in your wedding gown, or you can grab some comfy shoes and press start. Don't just indulge yourself in one more great idea about you and God. Ideas left without accountability and action are dangerous.

And that is where we end many of the books we

have read—with some great ideas. We love ideas, new thoughts, creative angles, forever wanting to be in motion. Intellectualism is a slow poison to our culture. I would hate for this book to get caught in that wave. It would be too easy to inhale all of these words and revealing ways to look at God anew—and do nothing about it. We could get lost in the pictures of the bedroom or pregnancy, even adultery and miss the heart of what God is trying to tell us. There is nothing new in this book. Everything has already been said. The picture of you and God being married is a total copy of what God's Word has already told us. The way we guard against intellectualism is practice. We actually work on what we are talking about, what we have been idealizing for the past ten chapters. It's the reason you picked up this book: to establish the "more" in your relationship with God … today.

> *And I pray that you, being rooted and established in love, may have power, together with all the saints, to grasp how wide and long and high and deep is the love of Christ, and to know this love that surpasses knowledge—that you may be filled to the measure of all the fullness of God.*
> -Ephesians 3:17b-19

God is longing for you. He longs to hear your voice, to see your face, to be in your presence. His longing isn't for what He can get from you or what you can do for Him. Come to the edge of all your frustrations, expectations, and disappointments – and allow your Husband to lift you to places beyond where your feet can walk.

> *However, as it is written: 'No eye has seen, no ear has heard, no mind has conceived what God has prepared for those who love him. For to us God revealed them through the Spirit; for the Spirit searches all things, even the depths of God.*
> -I Corinthians 2:9-10, NIV

The Holy Spirit longs to reveal all that God has prepared for you. Go on, wear the beautiful gown, vow your all to the Lord. But don't forget to wake up the next day and put on your jeans and live the life you were designed to live with Him—your MORE is waiting for you.

about the author

Irini is a wife and mother, teacher and student, speaker and listener. She and her high school love, Kenneth, have two children: Kalila and Warren. Her passion is to never let her heart settle for less than whole intimacy with the Lord, nor let others settle either. Out of that desire, her personal ministry, More Than, was birthed. She is also involved in a ministry that empowers women called Four Oaks. Irini is ordained through the Wesleyan Church and has her Masters of Divinity from Beeson Divinity School.

More Than exists to ignite, encourage, equip and empower the bride of Christ into a deeper intimacy with Him.

For more information or to book More Than, visit
www.bemorethan.com

Four Oaks desire is for women to seize and cultivate the land that is theirs through knowing God intimately, living securely in their identity, restoring their relationships, winning their battles, agreeing in their freedoms, receiving their empowerment, and living their destiny now!

For more information or to book Four Oaks, visit
www.4oaksonline.com